FOUL DEEDS AND SUSPICIOUS DEATHS
IN AND AROUND ROTHERHAM

Foul Deeds and Suspicious Deaths In & Around
ROTHERHAM

To Les

all my Love Daphne

Kevin Turton

Series Editor
Brian Elliott

Wharncliffe Books

First Published in 2003 by
Wharncliffe Books
an imprint of
Pen and Sword Books Limited,
47 Church Street, Barnsley,
South Yorkshire. S70 2AS

*For up-to-date information on other titles produced under the
Wharncliffe imprint, please telephone or write to:*

    Wharncliffe Books
    FREEPOST
    47 Church Street
    Barnsley
    South Yorkshire S70 2BR
    Telephone (24 hours): 01226 - 734555

ISBN: 1-903425-27-1

A CIP catalogue record of this book is available from the
British Library

Cover illustration: *Front -* courtesy of The Art of Mystery and Detective Stories,
                  edited by Peter Haining. *Souvenir Press Ltd.*
                  Rear – All Saints Church, Rotherham. *Brian Elliott.*

Printed in the United Kingdom by
CPI UK

Contents

Introduction

There are few circumstances in life where we would expect anyone other than our closest friends and relations to know anything of our existence. We brush past lives on a daily basis yet never reveal the nature of the sentient being we are or have become. Death is the only mechanism by which the veneer wrapped around our life can be stripped away. Even then, the exposure tends to be superficial. For we are almost always protected in death by those we know in life.

Murder and suspicious death changes this. When proved as a crime it is heinous, its impact upon those you have known devastating. Yet to those who have no knowledge of our life it is empowering. The very nature of either means disclosure must follow. Dissemblance is not an option. Lives are revealed piecemeal through both press and courtroom. The victim becomes public property in a manner never intended by the way they lived their life.

Yet we rarely feel animosity toward them. Instead we agonise over the disclosures, are harrowed by the detail and unnerved by the possibilities. We both accept and understand the need for such public exposure. The dissolution of a life is a price worth paying if a killer is caught.

Foul Deeds and Suspicious Deaths in Rotherham is a collection of true stories recounting the events that shattered a number of lives and for whom this dissolution is long past. It does, I hope, also give an insight into the society in which these people lived, the social conditions prevalent at the time and the manner in which the law handled those accused.

Forensic medicine is a relatively recent innovation. Until 1901 it was impossible to differentiate between blood types. Biologist Karl Landsteiner was the first scientist to discover that blood could be grouped as type A, B, or O; AB was not discovered until 1902. So prior to this, police were only ever able to determine blood staining as either animal or human. Serology, the modern means of distinguishing between these groups through identification of blood serum and its constituent parts, was not developed for a further fifty years. Following this has developed the science of DNA. We are therefore, far better today at determining the events surrounding a violent crime and identifying its perpetrator, than at any time in our history. All of which means criminal trials in our recent past could be extremely hazardous affairs.

Examining those cases that aroused such public interest in Rotherham's past has been a voyage of discovery, not only in the social history it uncovers but also in the changing attitudes to crime generally. In 1865 Rotherham's population was in the region of 19,000. Violent crime was less widespread than perhaps imagined. Therefore, crimes of this nature were widely reported, as were suicides and any death where suspicious circumstances suggested a third party involvement. In turn these created an avid readership for the press coverage they generated, more so murder, which often attracted large crowds to Rotherham's courthouse; the cases themselves being published in almost verbatim fashion by newspapers whose readership appears to have had a voracious appetite for close detail. By the outbreak of World War Two this began to change. Reportage became less detailed and by the fifties, when the town's population expanded to over 250,000, there are more headlines than known facts. So I am extremely grateful to the reporters of the *Rotherham Advertiser*, who over the years covered by this book, have created for the historian/writer a wealth of information and knowledge, though the task of combing their pages is a tedious one.

Does all this mean Rotherham has become a more violent place in which to live than it once was? Most certainly not. Crime in whatever guise has been a part of our society for the whole of history. What intrigues us, perhaps some would say in rather a macabre way, are the intertwining human relationships that are often the reasoning behind the most heinous of crimes. Agatha Christie, Patricia Cornwall, Reginald Hill, to mention but a few, could not exist if we were not beguiled by the characters populating their books. Characters, some of whom we know to be killers, whose complex personalities range from the diffident to the conceited and are the cause of our buying interest. True crime is no different.

In researching this book I found myself enamoured by some of the true life characters I feel I met, and filled with a sense of aversion to others I would have no wish to meet. The story of Annie Marriott, her baby and how society in 1891 treated her moved me considerably. So did the appalling tragedy of the double murder at Kimberworth. The strange death of Henry Cook left me wanting to know more about such an intriguing man who had lived through hardship in an area of Rotherham I knew so well from my own childhood; whilst the social deprivation of the thirties was brutally brought home to me as I uncovered the heart-rending story of Nora Taffinder. Real lives and real adversity.

Most of whom, I feel it fair to say, would have long since faded into obscurity were it not for Rotherham Library and in particular the staff of Rotherham Library's Local Studies and Archives section whose largess has known no bounds and whose meticulous attention to detail in maintaining accurate reference records is superb. My grateful thanks to all.

So, be moved to tears or riven by anger as you glimpse the lives of those who make up this collection of true events, but above all enjoy the journey.

Chapter 1

Highway Robbery and Murder – John Whitaker 1856

Johnohn Whitaker showed no outward signs of being a wealthy man. He lived a relatively frugal life despite owning and working his farm at Thrybergh. He had invested little money in the farm's outbuildings over the years and had shunned all suggestions to rebuild the dilapidated farmhouse he had occupied since his father's death.[1] In fact

Map of Thrybergh, 1851, showing what is believed to have been John Whitaker's Farm. Ordnance Survey/Rotherham Archives and Local Studies

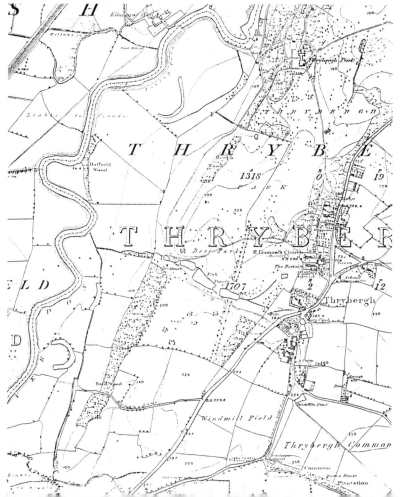

this appearance of impoverishment had given credence to local opinion that his general financial health was poor. This in turn made his occasional acts of generosity toward his neighbours more endearing to the community at Thrybergh than it did to the small circle friends who knew him well.

On 17 October 1856, as was his customary practice, he had been attending a cattle show in York. Having completed a number of business transactions with farmers from the north of the county, it had been his intention, at the end of the day, to catch the 6 pm train from York to Swinton. Here he was to have been met and taken home by horse and trap. Unfortunately, business took longer than expected to conclude and he missed it.

This meant being forced to catch the mail train, which only stopped in Rotherham, if he was to stand any chance of arriving home that night. Unwilling to stay in York, despite the hospitality offered to him, he decided to make the late journey in the hope he could find lodgings in the town. He finally arrived at Masbrough railway station at ten minutes past eleven that night, took a horse cab into Rotherham and arrived at the *Wheatsheaf Inn* on Doncaster Gate at a little after 11.15 pm. As a friend of the landlady and her family it was an obvious choice for a bed for the night. But business in Rotherham had been quiet for much of the day and the family had retired earlier than usual. After a short deliberation he decided to leave them in their beds and walked on to the *Pack Horse Inn* on Wellgate

Masbrough railway station. The Author

Doncaster Road, Thrybergh, c.1902-10. Rotherham Archives and Local Studies

to have a threepenny tot of gin and consider his next option.

York had proved particularly fruitful, as he had intended it to be. But in turn it also meant he was now burdened with the days proceeds of over £200 and most of that in cash. No doubt the thoughts running through his mind, as he stood at the bar that night, had more to do with its safe keeping than the distance he was faced with walking.

At a little after 11.30 pm he was joined by Mr Charles Nuttall who had also been to York and was driving a small group of cattle to Bramley. He offered John Whitaker company for part of his journey if he wished it. There was no hesitation in accepting the offer and the two set out for Dalton a few minutes later.

In later testimony to police Nuttall claimed to have seen two

The Grapes Hotel *where John Whitaker had hoped to find lodgings.* Author's Collection

men as they approached Dalton and the Bramley road turn off. Expressing concern at the amount of money John Whitaker was carrying and feeling uneasy about the men loitering ahead, he advised him to find somewhere to stay the night then finish his journey in daylight. Whitaker apparently agreed and said he knew Mrs Battersby, landlady of the *Grapes* at Dalton, who could put him up. So the two men parted.

But just as he had found in Rotherham the place was in darkness and again, as in Rotherham, he decided not to disturb their night. It was now just after midnight. There was no choice but to continue walking. As he reached Dalton Lane End, at the bottom of Winney Hill, two men, possibly the same two seen by Nuttall, stepped out of the shadows and blocked his path. There could have been no doubting their intentions, at that time of night, in that particular location. From the story John Whitaker related later that night he opted to retrace his steps out of Dalton and immediately turned his back on the two. Unfortunately, they were not alone. Unbeknown to him and obviously unseen by him were two others who now blocked the road behind him. The skirmish, when it came, was brief; quickly over-powered, he was savagely beaten about the head by what were termed in court as 'life preservers'. These were reinforced whip handles with lead weights inserted in the head, capable of inflicting tremendous damage, and were the favoured method of robbery assault. Once knocked down, the money was easily found, and placing a bag over his head the four left him lying in the road. There he lay for a least thirty minutes, unaware of his surroundings for most of the time.

As he recovered consciousness he could see, some 100 yards ahead of him, Miller's Windmill, a familiar sight at the turn of the century and reasonably well lit. It was here, after pulling himself to his feet, that he made for.

According to William Widdison, who kept a diary of the events, it was a little after 12.30 am when John Whitaker, blood still pouring from a series of head wounds, pushed his way through the unlocked door of the Windmill. Widdison immediately called out to his uncle, with whom he lived, and the two men brought him to the fire to better tend his wounds. After some few minutes the uncle then went off to rouse the neighbourhood, had a pony saddled and sent the two nearest neighbours to fetch the local Bobby from his bed at the police house in Rawmarsh.

Whilst all this activity was going on outside, John Whitaker responded to Widdison's ministrations and recovered sufficiently to insist on walking the rest of the way home. There was some debate between the two men along the lines of the wisdom of such a decision but John Whitaker was adamant. After some consultation with his uncle, William Widdison gave his assent but insisted on accompanying him. He also arranged for the doctor at Swinton, Mr Blythman, to be brought from his bed and sent to meet them at Thrybergh. At this point Whitaker realised both his watch and his keys had been lost in the attack and both men returned to the scene of the assault to try and recover them. Widdison recalled later how, after finding the keys and a fruitless search for the watch, he noticed how blood appeared to have formed, two pools either side of the road. Further evidence, if any were needed, of just how

Dalton Brook Mill, Doncaster Road, Dalton, where John Whitaker sought help after he had been attacked. Rotherham Archives and Local Studies

violent the assault had been.

Once back at the farmhouse in Thrybergh, a remarkable feat in itself, the housekeeper, Mrs Marriot was knocked up and within minutes of being admitted John Whitaker lost consciousness. Dr Blythman duly arrived and made a thorough examination of the wounds. His opinion was reasonably straightforward, from what was discernible he determined that if John Whitaker were not to regain consciousness within the next twenty-four hours then he would likely die. The diagnosis, despite its simplicity, was accurate. He never rallied and was dead within the day.

The funeral was at Thrybergh churchyard and he was buried alongside his parents on 22 October 1856. He was only forty-two-years-old. There were few mourners. John Whitaker, a bachelor, had never made friends easily. Though it transpired when the will was read that, contrary to local belief, he had considerable wealth, some £10,000, left to him by his parents and that the frugal life he had chosen to live

Thrybergh Church where John Whitaker is buried. The Author

had been incompatible with the amount of money available to him.

Despite police enquiries and some diligent work by the local constabulary no one was ever arrested or suspected of involvement. The case was quietly put to one side and placed in the unsolved files. There it would have remained had it not been for a public falling out between a man and his wife twenty five years later.

On Wednesday, 10 May 1882 police were called to the home of Ellen Leedham at Bailey Lane, Sheffield. It was 3 am. Outside they found her estranged husband, Aaron Leedham. He had already assaulted his wife and having been bound over to keep the peace for three months some few weeks earlier, was duly arrested.

The Leedham's had lived apart since 7 July 1881 and though their marriage had been a stormy affair their separation had been worse. Ellen Leedham claimed to have been living in fear for almost a year, but not simply because of the separation she had forced upon them, but because of something she claimed to have knowledge of. In the statement she made to police that morning she stated that her husband had been one of four men responsible for the robbery and murder of John Whitaker in 1856.

It took no more than twenty-four hours for word to spread and set the town buzzing with rumour and speculation. The murder of John Whitaker in 1856 had caused a deal of disquiet and those that could recall any detail of the robbery, remembered also that a reward of £200 had gone unclaimed. For a possible arrest to be made after so long a period was considered remarkable by most, not least because twenty-five-year-old murder cases, where police protocol was ineffectual at it's best, did not lead to much public confidence in police ability to pursue the case to a certain conclusion. There was good reason for their scepticism but for the time being it would be unfounded.

On 12 May Aaron Leedham was brought before Sheffield magistrates and bailed to appear one month later on the charge of assault. Superintendent Hammond, of Rotherham police, attended the hearing. He too knew the difficulties in building a successful case of murder and no doubt had intended interviewing Leedham were he to have been remanded.

On 13 May the *Rotherham and Masbrough Advertiser* published Ellen Leedham's statement in full. It simply added fuel to the fire, as it was probably intended to do. Superintendent Hammond, who must have sanctioned it's release, needed to find anyone with knowledge of the crime. By this time he would have been made aware of the fact that at the time of the killing the murder investigation was only handled by parish constables and, as far as could be ascertained, they took no written statement from any witness.

Knowing they were to hand over their responsibilities and area's of jurisdiction to the West Riding Police Force on 1 January 1857 no doubt had something to do with it. He was well and truly hamstrung, and forced to relaunch an investigation into a crime where many of those with information were probably dead. Allowing the statement out into the public domain, it was probably hoped, would find those that were living.

It certainly found William Widdison and his diary but, disappointingly, little else. The only thing in support of any charge of murder was the statement made by Ellen Leedham.

After suffering a year of abuse, both physically and mentally, she told Superintendent Hammond she had had enough. Despite involvement with the police over this time the attacks had not stopped. She simply wanted to be able to live her life free of violence and threat. Telling her story, she hoped, would remove him from her life and allow her to bring up her two daughters without this constant threat hanging over her.

According to the statement Ellen made, she was unaware of her husband's involvement in the murder until June 1881 when she asked that he visit her sister at Dalton Brook. He refused, there was an argument and he became distressed. She wanted to know just what it was that caused him so much anxiety over a visit to her sister and insisted he tell her. There followed a discussion about the murder of twenty-five years earlier. She asked him for an explanation and he, in turn, made his first admission:

> ...*Thah know'd Whitaker... well I helped murder him – me and a man named Siddall Bob of Attercliffe, who had a bulldog which we set at him first, and after all it was not worth our while, as he had only £90 and his watch. My father took the watch to London and when he died he left it to our Clara, who lives at Attercliffe.*

He then attacked her, beat her and threw her out of the house.

It was a short separation, she was back home within the day and the episode was forgotten until a few weeks later when, she claimed, the two met the man known as 'Siddall Bob' whilst in Castle Street in Sheffield. The three went for a drink and during the time they were together she recalled a comment Siddall Bob made appertaining to a watch and noticed her husband nudge him into silence. Once outside he confirmed to her this was the same man that had taken part in the killing. On 7 July 1881 after yet another violent outburst she left him.

John Whitaker's gravestone. The Author

On Sunday, 14 May 1882 Rotherham police arrested William Siddall, *alias* Sidley Bob or Siddall Bob in Attercliffe. On the following day Aaron Leedham was returned to custody and both men formally charged with the murder of John Whitaker. Both men denied their guilt.

Some five days later the Leedhams were brought together by police in the hope Ellen Leedham could convince her husband to confess his involvement. It was, to all intents and purposes, a difficult meeting but the following day he made a verbal confession to Sergeant Berry in which he allegedly stated that he, Siddall, his own father and an unnamed man committed the killing. The unnamed man he claimed was living abroad.

Twenty-four hours later he committed this statement to paper and made a full confession. This time he named the so far anonymous fourth attacker as a man he had never met before and knew only as Palframan. Now Superintendent Hammond had, what he considered, a true version of the events of that night. According to the statement, subsequently published by the *Rotherham and Masbrough Advertiser*, Leedham, who was only seventeen when the attack took place, had gone to the Grapes public house that night around 10 pm:

> *...a man named Palframan and Sidley Bob came in afterwards. They began to talk to father, but I could not hear what was said as they only whispered...Palframan kept going out and coming in the house during the evening... after a bit father and I left the other two men. Father sent me down the road to see if anybody was coming. I came back and said, 'somebody's coming like a farmer'. In a little time the man came past the place where we were and went on the road leading to Doncaster... Father, Sidley Bob and Palframan followed the man... Father was the first to strike him. He hit him over the face. Palframan and Sidley Bob then let go into him. They beat him about the head until he fell... my father lay across his face while Palframan felt in his pockets... After that Siddall and Father got up and walked away. Palframan shouted, 'I can't get away from him he's holding my leg.' My father turned back and gave the man a very hard heavy knock on the side of the head which knocked him flat.*

It was enough for Superintendent Hammond and the two men appeared at Commital proceedings at Rotherham Courthouse on the 22 May. But it was not enough for Mr Hickmott, appointed by the court to defend both prisoners at this committal stage. He argued strongly that the confession did not exist or that there was no evidence to support it having been made by Aaron Leedham. Justice Jubb, Chairman of the bench, insisted it was admissible evidence and could see no reason why it should not be used in court by the prosecution counsel. Prosecution at this time was not obliged to disclose their evidence to the defence. Nevertheless, Hickmott was incensed that a confession he claimed to have never seen could be admitted to the court. Prosecution counsel refused at that juncture to allow him access. Justice Jubb intervened and claimed he personally had read it. Hickmott could contain himself no longer and attacked the Chairman's right to view evidence before it had been presented to the court.

Mr Hickmott:	*...your knowledge ought not to extend to what you have seen privately. You come here in a public capacity, and in a public capacity you ought to know nothing beyond what is given in evidence.*
The Chairman:	*I ought to use my discretion in this matter.*
Mr Hickmott:	*Your discretion only goes so far as what you learn in your public capacity.*
The Chairman:	*It is not evidence against your client.*
Mr Hickmott:	*Yes it is evidence against one. There should not fall from your lips as chairman any such remark as you have seen the confession.*
The Chairman:	*I have seen it.*
Mr Hickmott:	*Then you ought to have evidence of it before you take cognisance of it.*

The exchanges continued throughout the afternoon sessions resulting in the prisoners being remanded for a further week whilst police enquiries could continue in an attempt to add validity to the confessions' detail.

In the week that followed little progress was made. Police were aware that at the time of the murder two life preservers (coshes) and a hat were recovered from the scene. None of these had been traced since the arrests of the two men. They desperately needed to find these items and believed that they were taken by some unknown retiring parish constable as a memento twenty-five years earlier. No written record of course existed and attempts to locate anyone involved in the original investigation had drawn a blank.

On 29 May, the prisoners made a further brief appearance in court and were remanded for a further week. Three days later the *Rotherham and Masbrough Advertiser* published an appeal for information. This in turn led to a further remand because police claimed new information had come into their possession as a result of appeals. This information would require close scrutiny. After prolonged objection by the defence counsel, who refused to believe the police could ever mount a serious case, the remand was finally granted.

On 11 June they were again brought before the court but this would prove the final time. The so called 'new information' had failed to materialise and police had to admit their inability to produce any corroborative evidence in support of Leedham's confession. The prosecution requested both men be 'remanded at large' which meant they could be released. Mr Hickmott was not satisfied. He knew only too well that to release the men under those circumstances meant they lived out their lives with a murder charge hanging over them. There was fierce debate between all sides of the legal divide, resulting finally in the Chairman of the Bench, Justice Jubb, who had listened to all the debate throughout much of the day, refusing to accept the defence plea. Taking instead the view that it was not beyond the realms of possibility that further evidence could be forth coming and because of that possibility the argument to 'remand at large' was a reasonable one. He also made the point that this decision would also mean releasing the men back into society and their families whilst at the same time granting to police the power to re-imprison them quickly if looked for evidence materialised.

Hickmott was immovable in his argument that to do so would also ensure the two men lived with the spectre of imprisonment and conjecture as to their culpability for the remainder of their life. To 'remand at large' was akin to a guilty verdict, he argued. But to argue semantics carried little weight.

The court decision not to pursue the two through a murder trial at this stage was upheld and they were were duly released. No charge of capital murder was ever forth coming.

Whilst it seems highly likely Aaron Leedham was part of the group that attacked and murdered John Whitaker in October 1856 and that his account certainly had the ring of truth about it; unless it could be proved, and that meant being able to produce supporting evidence that would both corroborate his version of events and convict Siddall, then a charge of murder stood little to no chance of proving successful.

The mysterious Palframan was never found and neither was the watch Leedham claimed to have been in the possession of his sister, Clara.

Chapter 2

Murdered for a Watch – John Coe 1880

On the morning of 19 February 1880 Samuel Bendin, milk seller, was half way through his working day, the time was around 7.30 am. As he walked along Canklow Road toward Rotherham he saw, lying up against a hay rick, what he thought to be a drunk who had slept the night in the open. He ignored him, as did James Hawthorne and Joseph Hawksworth who passed him during the next hour. At just after 8.30 am John and George Swallow, father and son, who both worked at Bentleys Brewery on the Whiston side of Canklow were about to do the same. Something in the way the man lay changed their minds and they decided to investigate. What they found was the dead body of John Coe, though his identity would not be discovered for several hours. They left it undisturbed and ran into Rotherham to fetch the police. By the time they arrived back the local *Advertiser* reporter was already on the scene.

According to the report he filed later that day the body lay on its back within the lee of a sandstone wall, the head pointing down the slope of the field toward Canklow Road, the feet in the direction of Boston Park. The face being indistinguishable because of dried blood covering most of the head. Across the forehead a long open wound exposed the brain and blood streaked the sides of the Hay Stack and most of the ground around where the body lay. Some five or six yards away lay a broken hedge stack and near to the stack a long stick, either were presumed to have been the murder weapon. By 9 am, attracted by the sudden police presence, a large crowd had begun to gather, their numbers gradually increasing as the morning wore on calling on more and more police to keep them away from the crime scene. At around 10 am the body was removed to the Rotherham workhouse for further examination by the Medical Officer of Health, Dr Julius Hardwicke. He confirmed the body had been struck repeatedly about the head, possibly by either one of the two lengths of wood found at the scene and that as a result the skull had been fractured.

Whilst this was ongoing, police were made aware of a man seen in the area earlier that morning and believed to be blood stained. The man was identified as David Coe, farm labourer, who lived at Brinsworth. Superintendent Gillett, who had taken control of the investigation, had Police Sergeant Morley take a horse and ride to Brinsworth to locate and arrest the man on suspicion. At a little after 10.15 am Coe was subsequently found outside the *Angel Inn* still walking home and taken into custody. It was the police intention to bring him before magistrates later that day but this proved to be a little over ambitious. David Coe was still inebriated from the previous night's drinking and was therefore locked in the cells to await the following morning.

Whilst he sobered up, Dr Cobban, Medical Officer of the Rotherham Burial Sanitary Authority, conducted a microscopic examination of the prisoner's clothing. His results found blood on the trousers, jacket and shoes. Closer examination of Coe's person discovered traces of blood smeared across his left hand. As the day came to a close all the blood found was confirmed as being human. Furthermore, police had been able to carry out a formal identification of the murdered man and from this ascertained that their prisoner was the deceased man's uncle. At that juncture it no doubt seemed an open and shut case. But things are often not what they seem.

On the morning of 20 February, David Coe, by now in a sober state, appeared before the Mayor, Alderman William Harrison and was immediately remanded into custody. On the afternoon of the same day the inquest opened at the workhouse on Alma Road, where the body had been taken after its discovery. There was little to add to the story already being pieced together by police but Dr Hardwicke was able to place the time of death at around midnight the previous night. Further information illicited from David Coe helped to build a reasonably accurate picture of the dead man's movements up until around 8.30 pm.

In the statement made by fifty-seven-year-old David Coe, once he had recovered from the previous nights excesses, he stated that both he and his nephew had been drinking for most of Wednesday, beginning in Wickersley, where they had gone early in the morning to watch the Earl Fitzwilliam hunt at Wickersley Bar. The afternoon had been spent in the *Mason's Arms* at Bramley where John Coe had entertained most of their fellow drinkers with a variety of music hall songs, something he had apparently become known for over the years. At just after 4 pm they arrived at the *Chequers Inn,* Whiston and there they were joined by John Henry Wood, *alias* Greaves, who had recently been released from prison after burglarising his own father's home. The three stayed together until 8 pm when it was decided to move on into Rotherham. According to David Coe his nephew had done most of the buying that day and when they all set out from Whiston as far as he could recollect, he still had quite a lot of money in his pocket.

Somewhere in the vicinity of Oakwood, David Coe, being a little more worse for wear than the other two, fell behind and was eventually left propped against a wall whilst they continued on without him. It was apparently some time later that he recovered, but only sufficiently to walk on to his sister's house on Clough Road, Rotherham, arriving there at around 9 pm. His sister corroborated the story and told police he had slept there until 5 am the following morning when, still somewhat inebriated, he had left her house and seemingly made the relatively short walk to the *White Swan Inn* at Westgate. Coe claimed he stayed there until after 7.30 am then set out on foot for Brinsworth where Sergeant Morley found him at a 10.15 am.

John Henry Wood, who quickly realised he was being implicated in the murder decided, of his own volition, to meet with Superintendent Gillett. Knowing the police house in which the superintendent lived he arranged the meeting for

The Belvedere *public house where John Coe and John Henry Wood went after leaving the drunken David Coe at Oakwood.* The Author

the evening of the 20 February. At this meeting he was able to substantiate much of what Coe had already told police and add missing detail relating to the murdered man's movements after Coe had been left by the wall. According to the statement he made, after David Coe had been left somewhere in the vicinity of Oakwood he and John Coe had gone on to the *Belvedere*, where they stayed for twenty minutes or so, then on to the *Mailcoach Inn*, Wellgate. Here he claimed they were joined by a woman he knew as Big Liz, otherwise Elizabeth Saunders. At around 11 pm John bought a gallon of beer and she, a woman named Annie Wilkes and the two men walked across the road to her house in a yard off Old Hill, Wellgate. By 11.30 pm, Wood claimed he and John Coe were walking back through Rotherham and parted company outside the *Mason's Arms*, Wood to return toward the Broom Valley area and John to walk towards Brinsworth village. That, according to his story, was all he knew of the affair.

It took a further six days of investigation to satisfy police that this version of events lent credence to the statements made by both David Coe and his sister. It was, therefore, decided on 25 February to release their prisoner back into the community 'remanded at large', which meant the charge of murder still hung over him but that most of his freedoms were restored.

The main reason for doing this were the various witness statements that had been taken during these intervening days which seemed to confirm Wood's version of events in relation to David Coe. No one had been found who could recall seeing him in his nephew's company after Whiston. Unfortunately for Wood, amongst these witnesses were those whose statements conflicted with that of his own. Reinforcing the growing police theory that despite his insistence to the contrary Wood had been very much involved in John Coe's murder. A warrant was subsequently issued calling for his arrest on 23 February. He immediately absconded. So whilst David Coe was being released, police were scouring woodland around Whiston and Morthen in the hope of finding traces of the man whose statement had helped release him but who was now widely believed to have murdered his nephew. Wood of course knew the search area well having spent much of his life on the farms dotted around both villages. Hiding out was less of a problem than finding food and it was this that finally forced him into the open. On 28 February, at 5.45 am, half starved and desperate for money to fund his fugitive status, he approached two men at Cotterell's Farm, Woodsetts, about four miles south of Worksop. After some discussion about casual work they sent him on to the farm. The farmer agreed to employ him for a few days and sent him back to the men he had just left with instructions they feed him. Manna from heaven for John Wood, except that this same farmer had recognised him from one of the various photographs in circulation, subterfuge being practised in order that he keep the hunted man on his premises whilst he set out for police at Laughton.

They in turn decided that in order to ensure an arrest could be effected without either a struggle or Wood's escape they would send two policemen in plain clothes back to the farm with the farmer. All three men arrived back at Woodsetts around 2 pm in a horse and trap, passing Wood rather fortuitously as they bumped their way along the narrow farm track leading to the farm house. Without stopping the two police immediately jumped to the ground and made what turned out to be a straight-forward arrest. Wood was tired, wet and beyond caring. By the end of that afternoon he had been arraigned before Rotherham's Mayor, Alderman William Harrison and by nightfall was safely in a cell.[2]

On 4 March, aware of Wood's arrest and imminent arraignment before the bench on a charge of murder, crowds started to build outside the Rotherham Court House. By 11 am when proceedings began there were 800 people packed into the public gallery and a similar number thronged outside hoping for some glimpse of Wood as he arrived at court, such was the public's interest in the case. During the course of that week the *Rotherham and Masbrough Advertiser* had displayed one of the many photographs of Wood now in circulation, in their office window. Taken whilst in prison for an earlier offence in November 1879, it clearly showed the wanted man in prison garb and caused hundreds to press their faces against the glass to better discern the man's features. There could therefore be no mistaking his identity then when he was eventually brought from the cells and placed into the dock. So disruptive were the crowd, and so overcrowded the courtroom, that proceedings were halted on three separate occasions causing Superintendent Gillett, on the last of those occasions to demand order or the court would be cleared. It had the desired affect and the rest of the day passed without hindrance.

From the start, the evidence produced by police, much of which had already been published, told a simple enough story of one man's intention to rob and his willingness to murder in order to carry out that robbery. Wood, impassive throughout the hearing, must have realised as each new witness took the stand and the clock ate up the hours, that his plea of not guilty was to carry little weight unless he could somehow disprove key elements of the story unfolding before the bench or his counsel discredit any of the witnesses who so damned him. Neither ever seemed likely.

With robbery cited as motive for John Coe's murder,

Pack Horse Inn, *Wellgate, 1898-1902.* Rotherham Archives and Local Studies

prosecution counsel told the court that though the dead man carried money, it was not simply cash that caused his death, it was his watch. What the press had never been told in detail was that the young man, apart from the coin in his pocket, had a silver Geneva watch attached to a length of steel chain, from which also hung a hard red stone encased in brass and used as a fob, along with a watch key. This very distinctive item, they claimed, would be the undoing of Wood. Seen by almost all the witnesses brought into court it had not been found on John Coe's dead body.

The story so faithfully reproduced by the local press was reiterated in court but with some important additional detail. After leaving David Coe the worse for drink somewhere in the vicinity of Oakwood, the two men had consumed beer in the *Belvedere*, the *Butcher's Arms* at the bottom of Moorgate and the *Pack Horse Inn* on Wellgate before moving on to the *Mailcoach Inn*. Here they were joined by a man named Thomas Wright at around half past nine. He had not been mentioned in Wood's account of the night but had been found by the police's witness appeal. He recalled the two were much the worse for wear when he first met with them but not roaring

High Street Rotherham, 1895-1900 by James Stansfield. Rotherham Archives and Local Studies

drunk. All three, he asserted, had walked on to the *Mailcoach Inn* at some time around 10 30 pm. When Elizabeth Saunders (Big Liz) and Annie Wilkes joined them at the bar, the man Wright, recalled that Wood carried a long, stout stick which had been shaped or wittled and resembled a rough walking stick. Annie Wilkes he remembered had tried in vain to get him to give it up and allow her to have it for her son. Wood had refused and did not relinquish his grip on it at any stage of the night. At 11 pm, when John Coe had bought the gallon of beer to take back to Elizabeth Saunders house, Wright had seen John Coe use the watch to check the time. According to the testimony of both women, none of which conflicted with that given by Thomas Wright, after arriving at the house John Coe became agitated and wanted to leave. At about 11.30 pm he went outside into the yard followed by John Wood and both men jumped the low wall leading back to Wellgate and disappeared. But they did not avoid being seen. A horse cab driver by the name of Holmes was awaiting his fare outside the Gentlemen's Club on High Street. The time was now twenty minutes to midnight and he could be precise because of the timing of the fare he had been booked to collect. According to his testimony Wood still carried the stick Thomas Wright had spoken of and the two were walking on toward Westgate. Some five minutes or so later he passed them at the bottom of Westgate where he was to drop his fare and watched them walk on toward Canklow Road. This totally contradicted Wood's version.

What followed next damned him. Apparently, on the morning following the murder, Wood had been seen by Robert Rotherham walking from town toward the *Stag Inn* on East Bawtry Road. It was 8 am. Frank Wadsworth (who met him outside the pub a little later) not only corroborated the sighting but also confirmed that Wood was wearing a silver Geneva watch at the end of a steel chain at the time. Evidence was then produced to show Wood had stayed at the *Stag Inn* for most of the day, informing the landlord he had spent much of the previous night in a shed owned by a farmer named Leedham somewhere between Rotherham and Broom Valley.

News of the murder apparently reached the bar at a little

The sandstone wall that once stretched from Boston Park to Canklow Road behind which the body of John Coe was found. The Author

after 11 am that morning. According to witness statements Wood took no part in conversations about the killing at that time. But at 12.00 midday he did enter into a conversation with a young man by the name of Charles Young. The man had walked into the bar at midday and instantly began speculating, along with the landlord, as to the identity of the murdered man found in a field near Canklow. Wood, who had taken no part in any conversation for most of the morning suddenly interjected with a question. He asked Charles Young if he knew of a man with one arm. Young asked if he meant the local postman, who fitted the description. Wood said no, the one-armed man he was referring to was related to the murdered man, the man Young and the landlord had been speculating about. It was a comment that would ultimately hang him. Police did confirm that a relative of John Coe had lost an arm. If, ran the argument, Wood had been in the *Stag Inn* since before the body's discovery, which he had, then he could not know the deceased nor to whom he was related unless he had been involved in the killing and knew the man killed. It was damning evidence.

But for Wood stood in the dock it simply got worse. Police were able to prove that after leaving the *Stag Inn* he met with a man named Robert Poynter. The two had a discussion about money and Wood offered Poynter a pocket watch. Poynter's description of that watch, a silver Geneva on a steel chain, added credence to the growing mountain of evidence that appeared to confirm Wood's involvement in the previous night's murder. For some strange, almost inexplicable reason, Wood allowed Poynter to keep the watch without any payment and this he did until he read of the killing.

On Saturday, 21 February he walked to Wood's parents house at Whiston where he knew Wood to be staying and gave the watch back. It was never found by police but an interesting aside was that Poynter told the court that in order to open the watch case he had had to use a knife and that the casing showed signs of having been opened in that manner previously. Needham's, the jeweller in Rotherham, confirmed in evidence that the watch he sold to John Coe, and had subsequently had returned for repair, also showed knife marks along the casings outer edge.

It was enough for the Rotherham Court and at 5 pm it decided there was sufficient evidence to send Wood to the York Assizes on a charge of murder. The trial itself took place over two days, 23 and 24 April. There was no new evidence and the jury took only twenty minutes to decide that John Henry Wood had committed murder. He was sentenced to hang on the Tuesday morning of 11 May. This was to comply with custom and tradition in York. Three Sunday's were to have elapsed before sentence could be carried out.

In an interview with the press on 27 April his father confirmed that whilst his son still protested his innocence, there seemed little doubt of his involvement. The trousers taken by police for blood analysis shortly after his arrest were not those worn on the night of killing. According to his father's statement, those had already been burned by Wood's sister because of heavy bloodstaining. The condemned man's contention was not that he had not been present at the killing but that he took no part in it. The killer, according to the statement made by his father, was a third man who had joined them at Elizabeth Saunders' house but who police had never found. Either way it carried no weight at this late stage.

John Wood, despite his public insistence that he was innocent, never mounted or supported any attempt at appeal. At 8 o'clock on Tuesday, 11 May Her Majesty's executioner, William Marwood, carried out the sentence. At that precise moment, in the small village of Whiston people gathered at the parish church and held a service of silent prayer, not in honour of the man but in condemnation of the act.

Chapter 3

A Question of Insanity –
Murder and Suicide
1883

oe Barker was a sick man. So said his wife Elizabeth when she called to see Dr Foote, the District Poor Law medical officer, in April 1883. According to Elizabeth her husband had begun to hide knives in the bedroom. She had been forced to develop a routine before she went to sleep at night which involved searching the rooms of the house before she felt safe to put the lights out. It was not a situation she felt she could cope with for much longer. Dr Foote in turn agreed, diagnosing the man as potentially suicidal or suffering a form of insanity. Joe Barker, without offering too much resistance, was refered to Dr Hardwicke, the workhouse[3] medical officer for a second opinion. After a lengthy examination it was decided he should be admitted to Wadsley Asylum, Sheffield.

Joe Barker stayed at Wadsley for four weeks during which time he exhibited a visible improvement in his condition. According to Samuel Mitchell, Medical Superintendent, since the time of his admittance he had showed few signs of neurosis. Within three weeks they were satisfied his period of apparent insanity had been brought about because of intemperance. No one could argue Joe Barker did not like a drink. Renowned amongst those who knew him well as a man capable of drinking twelve to fifteen pints of beer at one sitting, it was this capacity for alcohol which, according to Samuel Mitchell, had led to his mental instability.

For just over three weeks he had been put to work in the asylum gardens where he had proved himself an able and capable gardener. So much so that his constant requests to be allowed to return home were considered worthy of attention.

The Crofts, Rotherham as it looks today. The house facing down the narrow street is now a dentist, to the right of the house is the opening that once led into Barker's Yard. The Author

On 30 April he was brought before the visiting Justice's on whom the decision to release or not rested and it was decided to keep him for one more week. If all was well they all agreed, he could then be released. Joe Barker did nothing to blot his copy book, remained sober and on 7 May was duly returned to the family home in Barker's Yard, a narrow entry leading from High Street into the Crofts.

Elizabeth seemed satisfied with his apparent mental improvement and told friends and neighbours he was on the mend. Within two weeks of that home coming he had found work as a moulder at Masbro Stove Grate Works and all seemed to be well. Even William and John Cordron, with whom they shared their house felt he had recovered from the madness that appeared to be enveloping him. William was Elizabeth's father,

John her brother. The two of them travelled to work with Joe every morning at 6 am, if anyone was to recognise a resurgence of mental symptoms it was these two men.

Joe Barker though was far from well. Whilst those closest had not realised or had ignored the strange behaviour he continued to display at times, those who lived close by had not. According to William Tomlinson, a cab driver who shared the yard with the Barker family, he never considered the man to be anything other than insane. Since his release from Wadsley Asylum, he claimed, Joe Barker had constantly displayed signs of madness.

So, to some at least, there was no great surprise when he

The narrow entrance leading from High Street to the Crofts. Barker's Yard would have been on the right at the top of the short alley. The Author

attacked his family whilst they slept. On the evening of 1 June 1883 the family had retired to bed at their usual time. Elizabeth, satisfied her husband had recovered from his mental malaise no longer searched the rooms for knives. So the razor Joe Barker had slid under their bed went unnoticed.

The couple had five children aged eleven, nine, eight, four and two. Three of these children, the eldest, a boy named Edwin and his two sisters shared a bed in their parents bedroom. The youngest, Willie, slept between his mother and father. At just after 5.45 am on 2 June, Edwin awoke to see his father kneeling up in bed and drawing a razor from beneath the mattress. As he watched, his father leaned across the little boy lying in the centre of the bed and struck out at his mother with the razors open blade. At that precise moment she awoke. Turning herself away the slash was deflected by her shoulder. The second lunge caught her in the throat. Bleeding profusely from the open wound she rolled on to her side and out of bed. Once on her feet she ran to the three children at the other side of the room. Joe Barker caught her before she could rouse them from sleep and cut her again across the throat. Believing her dead he then turned his attention to Willie who still lay in the middle of the double bed but now wide awake. As he made to kill the defenceless little boy Elizabeth recovered sufficiently to throw herself at him and try to wrest the razor from his grasp. The fight that ensued was bloody and brutal resulting in Joe Barker cutting his own throat and Elizabeth Barker staggering from the bedroom clutching the razor only to die at the foot of the stairs.

William Tomlinson the nearest neighbour and Frederick Mason the local chemist broke into the house and carried Elizabeth from the stairs into a front room but there was nothing they could do for her. The chemist then went upstairs and carried each child down from the bedroom and out of the house. As police arrived detail of the killings was given by Edwin, the only witness to everything that had taken place that morning.

The inquest held at the *Three Cranes Inn*, High Street, Rotherham, before Mr Dossey Wightman, concerned itself in the main with hearing medical evidence with regard to Joe Barker's sanity. It was patently obvious from the crime scene and the young boy's testimony, which he repeated to the court,

Rear of Three Cranes Inn, *High Street 1928. This is believed to show Barker's Yard.* Rotherham Archives and Local Studies

that Joe Barker had committed murder. There was little doubt either that he was quite mad when he carried out the killing. The question the court wanted answering was why was he ever released from Wadsley Asylum?

After some lengthy debate amongst a variety of medical men, it was accepted that when he had been discharged on 7 May he had been sane. They could find no expert opinion to refute the suggestion release had been premature. But Edward Barker, his brother, told the coroner's court that Joe Barker had written him a letter on 8 May, twenty-four hours after his release from Wadsley Asylum. The letter which he produced to the court was unintelligible and in the main undecipherable. It was considered opinion that his brother was far from being anywhere near mentally stable when he returned to Rotherham. An opinion that was partially supported by a comment Dr Foote had made when the original diagnosis had been made. Diagnosis apart, he had told Dr Hardwicke that recovery could be considered a lost cause.

According to the Assylum itself they refuted any such suggestion. They were adamant their diagnosis was accurate and that Joe Barker exhibited no outward signs of insanity upon his release:

> There are 1880 patients in the asylum and we have them from periods of a week up to the length of their lives, according to the symptoms they show. It is not usual to discharge patients within the month. Barker was considered a sound patient.

Coroner Dossey Wightman decided their knowledge in medical matters certainly outweighed his own and so decided they must have been correct in their final diagnosis telling his jury,

> Joe Barker might have been in a fit and proper state to be discharged at the time he was from the asylum, and within a week or a fortnight after be in a state as bad as he was when he was sent, or even worse.

Still, they could not set up their opinions against those of the medical officers at Wadsley Asylum.

Unfortunately, Elizabeth Barker had no voice to be heard. Otherwise perhaps the view would have been somewhat different.

Chapter 4

The Murder of Baby Marriott
1883

Annie Marriott was twenty-one-years-old when she travelled from her home in Melton Browbray, Leicestershire, to take up a position of general servant for John Nicholas Archer.[4] She came with a good reputation, considered by both her previous employers to be, 'a most estimable domestic servant and above the average of this class'.

It was 6 January 1891, Annie had just spent a few weeks at her family's home and she was keen to be living away. She had good reason, for by the time she joined the household on Moorgate, Rotherham, she was six months pregnant. The Archers, despite Mrs Archer's suspicions, were not made aware of her condition. Annie feared had they known she would never have been offered the job. She was probably right.

All was well until Sunday, 1 March. At 8.15 am, as was her normal practice, she carried breakfast into the dining room for John Archer. He could see from the way she held herself that she was in great pain. There followed a brief conversation about her discomfort and she told John Archer her illness had started during the night. After serving the meal she made her way back into the kitchen where the pain became so great it caused her to scream out. John Archer found her in a partially collapsed state and told her to go upstairs and talk to his wife.

Some ten minutes or so later he found her in his wife's bedroom, apparently in less pain but still suffering from a great deal of discomfort. He heard his wife tell her to take fresh sheets from the linen cupboard and make up the bed in the next room and lie down. It was Mrs Archer's intention to get up from her own bed to help, but because she had been ill for a considerable time John Archer insisted she stay where she lay

Moorgate today. The Author

and he would do it. Telling Annie to stay where she was, he went off to make up the bed and then returned to help her into the room. He left her alone for a few minutes then knocked on the door to ask if she was all right? The pain by now had become severe and she asked if he would fetch a doctor. It was now around 8.45 am.

John Archer left the house to fetch Dr Branson who lived a

short distance away. The two men returned at 9.20 am. Annie still lay where she had been left. It took no more than a cursory examination by the Doctor to realise she had given birth. Dr Branson asked where the new born infant was hidden. She told him the child lay under her own bed in the garrett bedroom. He and John Archer then went up onto the top floor of the house and, just as Annie had said, found a child wrapped in a chemise, hidden beneath the bed. But this child had not just been hidden. Before pushing the baby under her bed Annie Marriott had slit its throat.

The baby had been a boy. The slash across its throat had severed all the main arteries and the windpipe. The child had died instantly and lost a considerable amount of blood most of which had soaked through the chemise and into the floor. Beside the body they found an open razor. John Archer believed it had come from a set of three which he kept in a drawer in the room. Dr Branson estimated the time of death as somewhere near to 8.45 am that morning. The child's body was still warm.

By 10 am that morning police were on the scene and the body removed for post-mortem examination. Annie made no attempt to hide her guilt and freely admitted to Sergeant Powell the detail of the killing:

> *I was ill this morning and Mr Archer sent me to tell Mrs Archer. I went and told her and she told me to go to bed and said that Mr Archer would fetch a doctor. I went to bed and the child was born. It moved two or three times... I got a razor out of the drawer and cut it. It did not scream. I put it into the chemise and put it under the bed. I came down and got into this bed.*

The statement was read to the coroner as the inquest opened at 10 am on Tuesday 3 March at the *Phoenix Hotel*, Rotherham. Chief Constable, Capt Burnett then requested the court be adjourned because Annie Marriott was too ill to attend and her family had yet to arrive from Leicestershire. It was agreed that because of her obvious distress she would be allowed to stay at the Archers' home in Moorgate for three weeks, by which time it was felt the

The Phoenix Hotel *where the inquest into the death of Annie Marriott's baby was held.* The Author

procedure could be dealt with on one day. The police were to ensure a presence was maintained at the house to ensure she did not abscond.

Yet within the week Annie Marriott was out of the Archer's house and installed in the workhouse on Alma Road. The Chief Constable was furious and letters written on 8 March bear out his anger at such a move being made. According to the workhouse the move was carried out at the insistence of Dr Branson who felt it best she be taken from the house and the police presence removed.

Either way, it did not prevent Annie from being charged with *wilful murder*. The inquest reconvened on 25 March and reviewed all the evidence in the case, of which little contradicted or defended her actions. It was a formality for the court to find her guilty and commit her to trial at Leeds Assizes.

The trial opened on 5 May before Mr Justice Day. The court was full, such was the interest her case had aroused throughout most of Yorkshire. Annie Marriott, pleaded 'not guilty' to the charge of murder. Under law at that time she was not allowed to give evidence in her defence but could only listen to the evidence against her as the day wore on. Fortunately it was to be a short trial. There was little to add to the evidence aired in Rotherham some two months earlier and the defendant had never denied her culpability. What was at stake was whether or not the jury would believe the killing of her child to have been as a result of momentary insanity or murder.

Defence counsel contested that Annie Marriott had not been aware of her actions on the morning of her son's death. They argued strongly that she was suffering from a condition of the mind medically termed, *Transient Delirium at the moment of parturition*. In essence, suffering short term insanity at the time of giving birth. They based their whole defence upon this one fact.

According to the Defence at her trial, Annie Marriott had returned to her garrett bedroom immediately after John Archer left the house to fetch Dr Branson. Not to commit a murder but to retrieve her night gown so that she would be more comfortable in the bed Mr Archer had made up for her downstairs. Whilst changing from her day clothes the pains she was suffering became so bad she almost involuntarily gave birth. At the moment of that birth and without realising why, she took a razor from a chest of drawers and cut the new born baby's throat. Then putting the body under the bed, returned downstairs to await the doctor. Mr Kershaw, on Annie's behalf argued:

> *In cases of murder one of the chief items is whether there was any premeditation of the commission of the crime. In this instance did not all the evidence point to the entire absence of*

premeditation? ...She did not conceal her condition from Mr Archer on the morning named, in fact she went to him and complained of being very ill, and that she had been in pain all through the night.... . The prisoner was practically alone in the house... could the jury imagine anything more tragic or touching than the state of this poor girl at that time. She had reached a supreme moment in a woman's existence, there was no-one by her to take her by the hand, and to speak a soothing word to her, but she was left alone in terrific agony of body and terrific agony of mind... .

It was an excellent defence even if there were little alternative. Though the judge, Mr Justice Day reminded the jury as they retired to remember:

The evidence left no doubt that the death of the child was caused with the razor by the act of the prisoner and any killing was prima facie *murder...*

It took the jury only thirty minutes to return to their place in the courtroom and announce their verdict of not guilty. Annie Marriott was discharged and released.

Chapter 5

A Falling Out –
The Murder of Samuel Barker
1904

Arthur Jefferies and Samuel Barker, *alias* Shiner, had once been firm friends. They were part of a well known poaching gang operating from the Holmes area of Rotherham. For reasons never fully explained, there had been a falling out in the summer of 1904 and Jefferies had been barred from the group. His protestations and verbal threats of violence toward those he blamed for his exclusion in turn, led to him being ostracised by most of the local poaching fraternity.

On Saturday night, 12 November 1904 at around 11.10 pm Samuel Barker was returning home after spending the night at a local theatre. Walking back to the Holmes area of Rotherham he met with his step brother John Broadhead outside the *Holmes Hotel* and the two were quickly joined by Frank Barker, Frank Strutt, Joseph Morris and John Greaves, all poaching associates, who had spent the night in various local pubs. After some banter they all began to walk along Holmes Lane toward their respective homes in the terraced streets off the bottom of Psalters Lane. As the group reached the fish and chip shop at the bottom of Belmont Street they were passed by Arthur Jefferies who purposely refused to acknowledge any of them. No doubt his lack of courtesy was understandable and the group reciprocated. After some few minutes stood around outside the shop they split and went their separate ways.

Joseph Morris, whose house lay across the courtyard known as No. 1 Court, Psalters Lane, had to turn into a passage leading from the street in order to access the courtyard beyond. As he reached the entrance to this passage way Jefferies and his wife stepped out of the shadows and asked him if he had seen their son, Bert. Morris said he had not, brushed past and walked on to his home. As he reached his own back door Samuel Barker in company with Strutt and Broadhead walked past the passage entrance on the street side, heading off toward Roseberry Street. Arthur Jefferies, who had remained in the shadow of the passage entry made an offensive comment to the group as they passed. Barker took immediate offence and struck out at him at which point Jefferies, grabbing at Barker's collar, dragged him into the passage. Broadhead made as if to follow but suddenly had his way barred by Jefferies' wife. Joseph Morris, hearing the sudden commotion outside, came out of his house in time to see the two struggling men emerge from the bottom of the passage-way into the courtyard. Barker gave a sudden loud groan and fell to the ground. Jefferies' wife let go of Broadhead and ran to her husband's assistance, falling over Barker's body as she did so. The two then turned tail and ran into their house. Broadhead along with Morris and Strutt then carried Barker, still alive but bleeding copiously, into Morris's home. A doctor was sent for but Barker was dead by the time he had arrived. One stab wound eight and a half inches long had penetrated the lungs and done the damage.

Police Constable Lewin Atkin,[5] oldest serving member of the force, took Jefferies into custody. By the time he was on the scene most of the Holmes neighbourhood thronged the street outside and obtaining any accurate assessment of events became virtually impossible. It was a little after midnight when he charged Jefferies with murder and because of the growing crowd outside had him taken to Frederick Street police station to better facilitate questioning. What he failed to do, as did those of a higher rank, was search Jefferies house until 2 am the following morning. Little wonder then no murder weapon was ever found.

The inquest opened and closed on Monday, 13 November without hearing evidence and set a date for reconvening on Thursday, 16 November. At 3 pm on the same day, crowds returned to the street to line the route of the funeral courtege as it wound its way through Kimberworth to the parish

Kimberworth, 1890-1900. The entrance into Psalters Lane can just be seen on the left. Arthur Jefferies funeral cortège would have wound its way from the top of Psalters Lane to the church, which can be seen in the distance. Rotherham Archives and Local Studies Library

churchyard, though it is doubtful if many of those in attendance had the slightest notion of the length of Barker's criminal record. He was clearly no saint, having over thirty convictions to his name, ranging back through his life to the age of twenty where he had been found guilty of drunkeness. From that point on, it could be argued he had been in a downward spiral, his offences growing in seriousness from poaching to assault.

On Friday, 18 November at just before midday, Arthur Jefferies stood in the dock at the Rotherham courthouse as the events of the previous Saturday were retold. He remained impassive as Dr William Henry Howthey described the scene at Psalters Lane when he arrived at 11.45 pm. According to his testimony, Samuel Barker was dead on his arrival. The later post-mortem confirmed he had been stabbed. The wound,

Kimberworth's Parish Church. The Author

some 8½″ long, penetrated both lungs and the aorta. It was the doctor's assessment that the instrument that caused this wound had to have been approximately twelve and a half inches long, three quarters of an inch wide and pointed.

There followed testimony from all the men that had been around Samuel Barker that night. No one was at variance with the statements they had made shortly after the murder except Joseph Morris. He stated that as he walked up that passage entrance and was stopped by Jefferies who enquired after the whereabouts of his son, he saw something glint in Jefferies' right hand. He was unable to define just what he saw but he believed it to be metal of some kind. Closely cross examined he told the court the object itself was no more than a third of an inch round and he could see some five inches or so of it. During the struggle he claimed to have witnessed that he only ever saw Jefferies left hand which was being used to grip Barker around the neck, or collar area of his jacket.

It was damning stuff. Jefferies had insisted since his arrest he had not killed Samuel Barker nor that he had any instrument, knife or otherwise that could have been used in the killing and police had found no murder weapon. The implication of Morris's testimony was huge. It not only showed culpability but intent. If Arthur Jefferies stood in that entry way armed then he had intended to kill or at the very least seriously wound his one time friend.

Its implication was not lost on the court. Other evidence supporting the idea that Arthur Jefferies had threatened violence in the past, simply added to the growing conviction

The Holmes Hotel *as it is today.* The Author

that he had intended murder that Saturday night. There was no evidence produced in mitigation. It was almost a forgone conclusion he would be committed for trial at Leeds Assizes. As the judgement was made a request for financial assistance under the *The Poor Prisoners Defence Act* was put to the court.[6] Unfortunately for Arthur Jefferies it was refused.

The inquest which had again opened and closed without hearing evidence on the 16 November reconvened finally on 23 November. It was singular only in that Jefferies, for the first time since his arrest, showed any real signs of collapse. Up until that point he had stoically refused to accept the seriousness of his position, believing instead that he could not possibly be found to have committed wilful murder. At the resumed inquest this icy cool façade finally cracked and he had to be taken back to the cells in a state of distress.

The following day he was taken by train to Wakefield prison to await his trial. The expected crowds never materialised, possibly because he was standing on the the platform at 6.30 am on a winter's day. Police made no attempt to handcuff him and he made no comments to waiting reporters who were the sole occupiers of the railway waiting room.

The trial opened on the morning of 8 December 1904. Arthur Jefferies had requested evidence from his wife and two neighbours be placed before the court to assist in his defence. The judge, Justice Grantham, having reviewed their evidence decided they had nothing to add to the defence case and refused to admit their evidence into his court room. This meant the defence had no witnesses to call that would support their contention that Jefferies was innocent of the charge of murder. The day had started badly.

Prosecution intended to show Jefferies had made threats against the poaching gang members since the falling out some months earlier. They made no attempt to explain the reasons behind this falling out. They did not need to. The men who made up that gang would offer enough evidence of implied violence or threat from Arthur Jefferies that the jury would be satisfied as to his intent. Long winded, unsubstantiated explanations of their cause were deemed unnecessary. All the men who had testified to the Rotherham committal hearing gave their evidence again with the exception of Joseph Beal. He had not been heard in Rotherham and had been brought to court because, as an old neighbour of Jefferies, he purported to have knowledge of the threats the prosecution made so much of. According to his testimony he had not only been in Jefferies' house when some of these threats were made but alleged to have seen the probable murder weapon:

> *...he had often seen him with an implement like a file which had been ground down for cobbling purposes. It was bright, and twelve to fifteen inches long. The prisoner flourished it and said it would do to use on one of the gang... .*

From that moment on the trial was effectively over. As the day came to a close and with no witnesses for the defence to be called, defence barrister, Mr Coutts-Trotter, asked the jury in his summing up to consider the act to be not murder but manslaughter:

> *The real question that I am going to submit to you, and I ask you to give it your earnest consideration, is this. Were there circumstances connected with this affray which would entitle you to say this was not a deliberate murder, but was the outcome of a struggle under circumstances which would reduce the offence to manslaughter. The way I put it is this: that you have these men obviously going to fight. I say obviously because Broadhead, the step brother of the deceased, told me quite frankly and openly that he had not the slightest doubt there was going to be a fight between them... I shall ask you to say there was a absence of premeditation and likelihood of a blow struck in hot blood which would entitle you to reduce the verdict to one of manslaughter.*

In his summing up Justice Grantham appeared to support the view that manslaughter had to be a reasonable possibility:

> *...if a man, having an instrument on him did not intend to use it, but was attacked by the other, or in the contest in the heat and passion and unintentionally, as it were, almost without being accountable for his actions, in the heat and passion used it. Well then, that would be manslaughter.*

He argued that because Jefferies had shown no singular animosity toward the man who died but toward the whole of the gang. Then it had to be a consideration that his actions were not premeditated. Had the police found the murder weapon and been able to bear out the testimony of Morris then quite possibly a different interpretation of events could have been made. Here he was scathing of police who had failed, miserably in his estimation, to find the murder weapon because they had failed to carry out a search of Jefferies house until 2 am in the morning. By which time, he argued, the weapon had been spirited away by one of those living within it.

It took the jury forty minutes to return a 'guilty of murder' verdict with a recommendation to mercy. Arthur Jefferies remained unmoved and had nothing to add to his defence before sentence was passed. He had probably been resigned to such an outcome from the moment he left the courthouse in Rotherham.

On 17 December *The Advertiser* editorial put the case for a reprieve. It argued forcefully that Arthur Jefferies had never intended to kill Samuel Barker and the fight was nothing more than a drunken brawl. The blow struck by Jefferies, they argued, had not been intended to kill. They supported the petition raised by Reverend Stock of Kimberworth and urged as many to sign as could. It was their contention that the jury's recommendation to mercy had been ignored by Justice Grantham and was still being ignored by the Home Office.

Yet it was clearly not an argument supported by all. There began a verbal battle between *The Advertiser* newspaper and one reader who in all his letters to the paper signed himself *JUSTICE*. So incensed were the editorial staff by his views they argued, after publication of the first letter, that the pen name ought to be amended to read VENGEANCE. So contrary were the views he expressed to those the newspaper promoted. But he refused to be cowed, arguing strongly that Arthur Jefferies was a murderer, whose chosen life had led him to commit an act that was, in his opinion premeditated. As for those of prominence signing their names to the petition....

A view of Psalters Lane looking toward the Holmes area of Rotherham. The Author

If these sympathetic gentlemen had given their time and trouble and contributions to a Santa Claus fund to provide and distribute a few thousand toys and boots or shoes to the poor and needy children of the town, I think they would have had a much worthier object to work for, and given greater happiness than reprieving half a dozen Jefferies...

No doubt his views carried weight with a number of people and whilst the petition rallied support it did not do so in any great number.

On Wednesday, 21 December a petition bearing the signatures of 3,300 local people many, as the reader letter indicated, of prominent men in the town, was formally handed over. It took only five days of deliberation to reject its assertion that the sentence be commuted to life imprisonment. Arthur Jefferies was informed of the decision on Boxing Day.

In a letter he wrote to his wife on the same day he sent thanks to those that had aided his cause and seemed resigned to his fate. He was duly executed at 8 o'clock on 28 December. There were two executioners, Billington, the Queen's executioner and his apprentice, Henry Pierrepoint.

Chapter 6

A Lover's Quarrel –
The Murder of Jane Hurst
1904

John Thomas Kay moved to 224 Sheffield Road, Ickles, in September 1902 with his wife. At the time he was foreman at a cutlery factory in Sheffield, earning a regular wage and the move was intended to be short term. Life had never been easy but over the years they had managed to bring up one child and accumulate some nice pieces of furniture which more than compensated for the decaying appearance of the cottage they had moved to.

One of three, it had been purpose-built for the brewery which once occupied the site but like its neighbours, had been run down since the brewery disappeared. Downstairs consisted of a small lounge, an even smaller kitchen and upstairs two bedrooms. Because of the thickness of the walls each window formed a recess into the interior rooms narrowing the amount of light each room received. As a consequence the house inside always had a gloomy appearance.

In October 1903 John Kay's wife died. There followed a long period of unhappiness during which he took to drinking more than was usual and possibly as a consequence lost his job. At some point toward the end of 1903 he met Jane Hurst and she moved into the house in January 1904. Previously married to a publican who, since their break up, had moved to Cardiff, she was in receipt of an allowance which he sent on to her every week. This was needed by both because of John Kay's unemployment. Unfortunately, once her husband became aware of her circumstances the allowance stopped and they had to resort to selling off the cottage furnishings to help pay the rent and buy food.

At some time in mid-March Kay took a poorly paid labouring job to help make ends meet. Here he met a young labourer looking for a room to rent. Kay offered him a bedroom and he moved in on 1 April. Five days later Kay, who should have been working a night shift, found Jane Hurst and his lodger sharing the same bed. After the row that followed the lodger was thrown out and Kay refused to go back to work, choosing instead to remain unemployed.

By the Spring of 1904 the strain on their finances was becoming desperate as were Jane Hurst's drinking habits. By this time neighbours had grown accustomed to not seeing her for days, though whether through drink or choice they were never too sure. What remained constant was John Kay's ability to find her again and bring her back to the cottage.

On Monday, 9 May, she had been missing for four or five days when Kay finally tracked her down and brought her back at 10 pm that night. There were no quarrels, no fights, nothing according to neighbours to suggest this was any more than the usual kind of episode. But that night John Thomas Kay snapped.

In the early hours of the following morning he awoke to hear voices in his head telling him to kill her. He calmly walked downstairs, found a hatchet, walked back up to the bedroom and struck her four or five times. The blows shattered her skull and scattered blood across the walls and ceiling of the room. He left her, still alive, and calmly walked into Rotherham with the intention of giving himself up to police at Frederick Street police station.

Kay's problem as he entered Rotherham was that he had no idea where Frederick Street was. So, to quote an old cliché, he asked a policeman. The policeman in question was Sergeant Brookes who had spent much of the night investigating a burglary and wanted to go home. It was 5.45 am when John Kay stopped him in Effingham Street to ask directions and it had been a long night. So he asked the obvious question, why? received no answer, so offered to walk with him. On route, after a little cohersion, Kay admitted his reason was murder, that he had killed his partner earlier that morning, saying 'I hit her three or four times, I don't know how many'.

College Square by E L Scrivens, looking down Effingham Street where John Kay met with police sergeant Brookes. Rotherham Archives and Local Studies

After locking Kay in a cell Sergeant Brookes and the desk duty PC, the only available policeman in the station, took the door key Kay offered and made their way to Sheffield Road. The scene upstairs was one of carnage. The bed, bedding, pillows, walls and floor were saturated in blood. The murder weapon, an axe, had been carefully placed where it could easily be found, on top of a box on the bedroom floor. Sergeant Brookes sent his PC off to the nearby Steel Peech & Tozer works where he knew there was a telephone and the police surgeon was sent for. Dr Wetherbe duly arrived, a little after 7.45 am. Jane Hurst, despite her appalling injuries, still lived though her breathing was shallow. There was no doubt she had never been aware of the attack and within the hour she was dead.

The inquest opened at the *Pheonix Hotel* the following day before a large crowd. The evidence was sparse, Kay had admitted the killing and Dr Wetherbe confirmed that five blows had been struck to the head, one of which destroyed the right side of Jane Hurst's brain. Kay remained impassive throughout the short hearing and showed no signs of emotion when the court declared *wilful murder* against him.

There were no large crowds at the funeral at Rotherham Cemetery on Saturday, 14 May. There were only three mourners, Jane Hurst's husband Thomas, who had travelled north from Wales, her son Frank and a friend of the family. Most would be onlookers who had been led to believe the funeral would have taken place in Sheffield so stayed away. The small family group had also arrived early in order not to arouse any public suspicion and were already in the cemetery grounds when the coffin arrived.

Thomas Hurst stayed in Rotherham after the funeral and attended the committal proceedings at Rotherham Courthouse on the following Tuesday. There was little added to the detailed description of events that had been presented to the inquest some six days earlier. Only evidence from neighbours, particularly Elizabeth Robinson, who had lived three doors away was new. In her evidence to the court she told of how, on Easter Monday, some three weeks before the murder, the couple had fallen out after a blazing row. The result of which was Jane Hurst being roughly manhandled and thrown into the street. According to her version of events Jane had spent that night at another neighbours house. The argument was patched up but Jane Hurst, as a direct result of that falling out, was making plans to leave Kay at the first opportunity. What she was unaware of at the time was that John Kay had made the same decision. In fact he had gone one stage further and ordered a dray to be at the house on the morning he committed the murder to collect the furnishings. Police confirmed that whilst Kay was in the cells and the body being removed, a dray did in fact arrive with instructions to remove what furnishings were left in the house. Police refused the driver access and sent him on his way. This simply compounded the evidence against Kay and there was little room for manoeuvre by the court. It came as no surprise to any attending, least of all Kay himself, that he was to stand trial at Leeds for murder.

The trial opened on 29 July before Justice Channell. Kay, because he had no money, had been unable to hire a solicitor to work on his behalf in the intervening weeks. It was to prove damning for his defence. The court had instructed Mr

West Riding Court House, College Square, by J Crowther Cox. Rotherham Archives and Local Studies

Mitchell-Innes to act as his barrister. It was his contention that John Kay had suffered from 'impulsive insanity' at the time of the murder. In other words he was temporarily insane when he struck Jane Hurst about the head. But, due to Kay's poor financial situation, Mitchell-Innes, by his own admission to the court, had been unable to take any instructions from an acting solicitor working on behalf of the accused. It meant the defence had little depth when it came to trying to substantiate the notion of insanity.

After the witnesses, first heard in the Rotherham Courthouse, had all filed into the witness box one after the other, Mitchell-Innes called Dr Clarke, Medical Officer to Wakefield Prison. He was the only medical witness available to him to add credence to the defence that insanity was the cause of the murder. It was to be less than successful. Though Dr Clarke did agree 'impulsive insanity' could have caused the voices heard by Kay and could have caused him to commit murder, he had found no evidence in his examination of his prisoner to substantiate the theory that he was, in any other medical sense, insane. Mitchell-Innes pressed the point that it did not matter if he was declared sane now, what mattered, he argued was that he was insane when he killed.

Mitchell-Innes:	*...would the fact that the man in question obeyed those voices without hesitation point to the fact of his mind being unbalanced?*
Dr Clarke:	*Unquestionably.*
Mitchell-Innes:	*Without hesitation as to right or wrong?*
Dr Clarke:	*Unquestionably.*
Mitchell-Innes:	*Now we have been told in evidence that to all appearances when this man gave himself up to police he was perfectly calm and clear. Is that consistent with his shortly before having committed a deed of violence under the influence of impulsive insanity?*
Dr Clarke:	*Yes sir, quite.*
Mitchell-Innes:	*And it is equally consistent, doctor, is it, with the existence of compulsive insanity shortly before that his memory was sufficiently clear to describe in some detail what he had done?*
Dr Clarke:	*Yes.*

But this was not an argument Justice Channell was going to accept. He had asked a number of questions throughout Mitchell-Innes cross examination of Dr Clarke and when the Doctor told the court that during his incarceration at Wakefield, Kay had made a statement to the effect that he had attempted suicide some two days prior to the murder, the judge questioned him about the testing techniques used to prove insanity. There followed a debate around what psychological tests were available to substantiate the developing theory being put to the court. Addressing the Doctor, Justice Channell sought clarification as to whether or not Kay exhibited any signs of the insanity the court was being asked to accept.

Justice Channell:	*I have written down your answer to questions as follows, 'I am unable to suggest any mode of testing whether the man's statement of hearing voices is true other than the man's manner in giving it. It was the clearness of it, the want of hesitancy, repeating the same thing without variation, the consistency of the statement at different times.' What do you say about that ?*
Doctor Clarke:	*The consistant statement at various times of the occurrence. I say that has a tendency to enable me to form an opinion as to the correctness of the statements he made.*
Justice Channell:	*Then am I right in understanding... other than his statements to you about what had happened on that particular occasion and about trying to commit suicide, other than those statements, you had no indication at all of insanity*
Doctor Clarke:	*That is so.*

It effectively killed the defence case. If it was impossible to prove John Kay heard voices or to validate the statements he made about those voices then insanity was extremely difficult to argue as defence. In his summing up to the jury Justice Channell made it crystal clear that to accept the argument of impulsive insanity was tantamount to granting every criminal that appeared in his court a mitigating defence.

Suppose a man of ability committed a murder and was enable to say, 'on this occasion I heard voices impelling me to commit this. I have never heard them before or since.' It opened the door for everyone to get off.

It took the jury only twenty-five minutes to agree with him. John Thomas Kay was found guilty and sentenced to death

At 8 o'clock on 16 August John Thomas Kay walked calmly to his death. Throughout his incarceration in Wakefield gaol he had never exhibited any outward sense of fear or remorse. He had been resigned to his fate almost from the moment he boarded the train in Rotherham to travel to his trial. In a brief meeting with what little family he had left, a sister, whom he had not seen for eighteen years, his daughter and his two grandchildren, he had only one tinge of regret. That he should have arranged for the drayman to have arrived on Monday to collect the furniture, not Tuesday, had he done so Jane Hurst would have lived. No doubt her family shared the sentiment.

Chapter 7

The Suspicious Death of Henry Cook 1906

Seventy-year-old Henry Cook was a strong swimmer. He had, over the years been known for his prowess in water, be that inland or sea. On 27 February 1906 he had walked into Rotherham from his home at 2 Bradgate Lane, Bradgate, as was his usual custom. He owned property on Wortley Road and called there as part of his journey. Extremely keen on instrumental music he liked to stand on Forge Lane listening to the Rotherham Borough Band as they played in the band room which looked out on the Sheffield and Rotherham Navigation Canal.

A joiner and undertaker, he had lived his seventy years in Kimberworth and Bradgate. As a young man life had been extremely harsh, his father dying whilst he was very young. But his mother had proved a resolute woman and as the young Henry Cook grew she had him apprenticed to a carpenter allied to an undertaker business. Here he was taught the skills

Bradgate Lane, Kimberworth, 1900. Rotherham Archives & Local Studies

The canal at Forge Lane where Henry Cook listened to the Rotherham Borough Band as they rehearsed. The steps referred to at the inquest were removed some years ago. The Author

of the joinery trade and in later life took the opportunity to purchase the undertaker business that had used his skills. Life, he would no doubt have argued, had been very successful. Over time he was able to attain a position of high regard amongst the community that knew him. A poor steward for the Wesleyan Church at Kimberworth, he had also worked as superintendent of the Sunday school for a number of years, held the post of church treasurer and was trustee of the Chapel. Marriage had proved as equally rewarding as it had long lasting, bringing with it a son and daughter both of whom had followed their father's example of success.

So on that cold night in February as he stood listening to the band from his vantage point beside the canal it could be said he saw himself as a very contented man. A man for whom life held real value and purpose. When Henry Rooks, a neighbour from Bradgate who knew him well, shouted hello to him from the opposite end of Forge Lane, Henry Cook was so enamoured by the sound of the band that he failed to hear. So when his body was found on the steps of the Navigation Canal at twenty minutes to six on Sunday morning by a policeman who believed he had drowned, no-one believed it.

The inquest opened on the following Monday, 29 February, at the *Old Gate Inn*, Bradgate. Deputy Coroner Mr J Kenyon Parker presiding. According to the testimony of the officer who had discovered the body, Henry Cook had been found fully clothed and partially wet. He lay across the first and second steps of a flight of stone steps leading down into the water, but on the opposite side of the canal to that on which he had stood listening to the band music.

The most obvious area to explore was that of suicide. Being found where he had highlighted the possibility that he had thrown himself into the water, possibly then having a change of heart. As a strong swimmer he could have extricated himself by swimming to the opposite side of the canal and climbing out. But this was not a view borne out by evidence from Henry Cook's own GP. He told the court that at no time had he seen any signs of neurosis or depression. In his opinion there had been nothing in Henry Cook's demeanour or physical make up that would have suggested suicidal tendencies. Having seen his patient on the Friday prior to his death he felt confident in his assessment that the man had been hale and healthy, except for a few minor ailments common to old age.

This view was reaffirmed to a large extent by the post-mortem results. According to doctor Collinson, who carried out that post-mortem, Henry Cook had sustained bruising to both legs and his left arm, otherwise he had been in rude good health. He had certainly not drowned. Evidence produced by the doctor in court suggested death due to shock. But this conclusion was by no means certain. When Mr Kenyon Parker asked the crucial questions the answers were less than satisfactory:

Kenyon Parker:	Has he died from drowning?
Dr Collinson:	No.
Kenyon Parker:	Then what has he died from – shock?
Dr Collinson:	I think so.
Kenyon Parker:	Had any of these bruises anything to do with his death?
Dr Collinson:	Not at all.
Kenyon Parker:	Can you express an opinion of how they were caused? Would they be likely to be caused by scraping against stones?
Dr Collinson:	They might have been – yes. I mean to say one cannot say.
Kenyon Parker:	They might have been caused by a great many things?
Dr Collinson:	Yes.

So the Deputy Coroner returned to the medical evidence Dr Collinson had given earlier in support of his argument against drowning paying particular attention to the state of Henry Cook's internal organs. He wanted to be sure beyond all reasonable doubt that Henry Cook had not drowned. Here Dr Collinson was on certain ground. The testimony he gave was as comprehensive as it was conclusive. Apart from a little fluid in the lungs the heart was in good condition, the stomach contained remnants of undigested orange and the larynx was quite free. All of which meant the man had most definitely not drowned in the canal that night, of this Dr Collinson was quite certain.

So why was he found on the opposite side of the canal to that which he had clearly been seen earlier? Police Sergeant Brookes[7] gave evidence to the effect that he could not have walked around to the other side of the canal because to do so meant having to walk through the lock house gardens. At the bottom of which and tied to a shed, was a dog. Furthermore a dog he and most that lived nearby knew well. Used by the lock keeper to alert the house to any that came near it would, in the sergeant's opinion, have tried to tear down the shed if Henry Cook had gone anywhere near it. He was of the view that the man had simply fallen into the water on one side and swam across to the other side, dieing as he hoisted himself out of the water. The only note of caution he made against this hypothesis was again the dog. It seemed reasonable to assume, he argued, that had he fallen he would have cried out for help. Yet no-one heard a sound that night and the dog never barked. The Deputy Coroner asked him if, when found, the man's clothing showed any signs of disarray. It had not. Henry Cook lay as he had stood that night listening to the band, fully clothed, his overcoat tightly buttoned up against the cold.

Inspector Gower supported his sergeant's prognosis despite having some misgivings. He was of the opinion that there was always a current of sorts in the canal, had Henry Cook gone into the water it would have assisted him in any attempt to swim to the other side. There was also a second piece to this reasoning, the steps near to where he had been known to have been standing were just short of touching the water, whilst the steps upon which he had been found dropped down below the water level. These steps were certainly the easier to use if trying to climb out of the canal. But as Deputy Coroner Kenyon Parker pointed out, were that the case surely the lock house occupants or their dog, would have been roused. Particularly, he pointed out, between 7 pm and 8 pm which Dr Collinson had judged to be the approximate time of death, based upon scientific evidence and which also fit his known routine of normally arriving back in Bradgate by 9 pm at night.

In discussion with the jury through it's foreman, Henry Hall of Manor Farm, Kimberworth, the jury expressed a view that he could have been in the water at some point that night and shock, as Dr Collinson had so cautiously concluded, could be a reasonable conclusion to arrive at. However, they were not satisfied that the evidence produced had shown how or why he would have entered the water. Neither was the Deputy Coroner.

He expressed a view in his summing up of the evidence that whilst it could be argued Henry Cook had been in the water at some stage of that night, he felt it highly unlikely to have been in the early part of the evening. Evidence suggested he would have been seen, most certainly heard and quite possibly rescued, were that the case. The occupants of the house which backed onto the steps upon which his body had been found, seemed sure they would have heard anyone calling out. Their dog most certainly would have raised the alarm, if, as sergeant Brookes had asserted, it was an animal known for it's ability to rouse the neighbourhood at the slightest hint of noise or commotion. He told the court that having heard all the evidence none had been shown to clearly prove or disprove any theory offered in solution of the mystery. Henry Cook had certainly not committed suicide, neither had he drowned in the canal, there had been no heart attack and no marks remained on the body conducive with the man having been attacked.

What happened to Henry Cook of Bradgate was simply not known and remains a mystery.

The Chapel at Bradgate. The Author

Chapter 8

Killed Over A Hat – Tom Tingle
1911

Thirty-three-year-old Willie Samuel Felton had suffered from a persecution complex for most of his life, believing, probably since his early years that he had been picked on or bullied in everything he ever attempted to do. Willie was suspicious of people, regardless of who they were and viewed most with a degree of distrust. He had moved to Yorkshire from Lancashire in 1901 transferring his skill as a miner to Wath Main where he remained for ten years. In 1910 he decided to achieve an ambition he had always fostered, to work for himself. He was thirty-two-years-old. Buying two horses and a cart he set himself up as an agent to ferry freight across town.

Initially he proved successful but within a year his business was in decline. He lost the first two horses in quick succession and toward the end of 1910 was fined for cruelty to a third. He obviously found tending horses to be an arduous task and as a consequence neglected their upkeep. In January 1911 he was struggling financially and both he and his wife, along with their four children were finding life less than profitable. Yet there was precious little sympathy emanating from those that knew him. They seemed to view his decline with a deal of jocundity despite his ever worsening financial situation. Had he not been so vocal in his condemnation of life and its inadequacies, particularly in relation to his own luck, perhaps it would have been different. As it was sympathy had given way to apathy and he was no longer being seen as a man struggling against the odds, but as a man devoid of any ability that would ever enable him to turn those odds to his advantage. For someone who had spent much of his life beset by self doubt it

High Street, Wath, by E L Scrivens, 1910. Rotherham Archives and Local Studies

Wath today. The Author

only added to his growing sense of paranoia.

On Monday, 30 January 1911, after an intended deal with horse traders had gone wrong, Willie Felton went out drinking. He had reached the lowest point in his life. Despite his best efforts he had been unable to rescue his business from the spiralling decline that had beset it throughout the winter. It was a turning point. For four months he had stayed away from alcohol in all its guises, believing sobriety to be a virtue that would lead him to solvency. As a philosophy it had proved woefully lacking. It seemed to Willie Felton as he set out that night, there could be no further virtue in remaining sober. Being a teetotaller had produced no advantage.

As a member of West Ville Working Men's Club in Wath he decided this would be where he began his new life. Arriving at around 7.30 pm that night and already in poor spirits, he began to drink. Within the hour a combination of alcohol and despair had turned him into a crotchety, quarrelsome individual who would brook no criticism from any quarter.

West Melton WMC, known locally as West Ville WMC. The Author

After bemoaning his bad luck to any as would listen, telling all he had only earned 1s 7d [8p] that day but had spent 7s [35p], he became abusive. Part of that abuse he directed toward the Club's committee members, criticising their lack of foresight in not viewing him as a potential committee member and comparing their opposition to his acceptance with that of the committee of Wath and West Melton Working Men's Club whom he felt to be equally incompetent. Between the two, he proclaimed loudly, they had conspired to keep him out, they were all against him. By 8.30 pm he had been shown the door and told to do his drinking elsewhere.

Yet, despite all of this verbal censure, it was to Wath and West Melton WMC that he went. Here were others he knew, others he hoped would give him a sympathetic hearing and buy him a few beers. He made straight for the games room and the card school he knew would be in full swing. There was no reticence from the group, he was readily found a chair and settled down to play cards, Solo Whist, for beer. But despite his best efforts he found it difficult to settle. Concentration, normally the mainstay of his game, eluded him. He lost most of the games he would normally have been expected to win and by half past ten was playing so badly those around him told him to go home.

He took little persuasion. Refusing the next hand of cards he left the room with Joe Fleming, one of the card school, a man who had helped him financially in the past and whom he trusted. The two of them held a brief conversation at the bar and Felton told him he was off in the morning to sell his horses and the cart at what was known locally as the Quarterly Sale. The brief flirtation with business was over and he would now look for work. As those sitting around the table shouted impatiently for Felton to go, Joe Fleming returned to the group. Felton made an angry retort and walked out of the room.

At this point it had been his intention to go home but seated at a table near the exit he saw John Williams. He knew Williams as a committee Member who had recently been re-elected to the Club committee and could not resist the temptation to criticise his appointment. Walking over to where he sat he

Wath WMC. The Author

made a disparaging statement about both him and other committee members. Williams told him in no uncertain way that if he persisted in that manner he would have him thrown out. Before Willie Felton had chance to answer another committee man, Tom Tingle, possibly in an attempt to diffuse the situation, walked up behind Felton and jokingly knocked his hat from his head. For Willie Felton it was the height of ignominy. Retrieving his hat from the floor he told Tingle:

I'm going to the corner, we'll see whether tha'll knock it off agean when I come back.

He then walked over to the corner of the room turned around, walked back and sat down beside Tom Tingle who had joined Walker at his table.

Tha knocked my cap off when I went out. Knock it off now.

Tom Tingle, not realising the threat Felton posed promptly did as asked. Felton immediately turned on him and appeared to strike him once. It took a moment before those around the table realised he had actually stabbed Tingle in the neck. Williams immediately stood up and grabbed at Felton's wrist eventually wrestling the knife from his grasp. Tingle in the meantime fell to the floor bleeding profusely from a wound that had severed his jugular. He was dead within the hour.

Dr George Hall Johnstone, a local Wath GP, was on the scene within minutes and had done what he could but there was no hope from the moment the knife penetrated Tingle's neck. The wound itself was not deep, five eighths of an inch, no more, but enough to severe the internal jugular vein. An injury that showed the great amount of force Felton had used in his attack.

As futile first aid was being carried out on the floor, not six feet away police sergeant Hirst, who walked his beat through Wath, was making the arrest. Felton made no apology for his actions whilst all this was going on and to prevent further trouble he was bundled out of the Club and taken to Wath Police Station some 250 yards away. Because of his inebriated state he was placed in a cell where he promptly fell asleep until after four o'clock in the morning and was not formerly charged with murder until half past eight. According to Willie Felton he had no recollection of events from the moment Tingle knocked the hat from his head until he awoke in the cells that morning.

The inquest opened at Wath-upon-Dearne Police Station at half past two on Tuesday, 31 January. Willie Felton was brought to the hearing by horse cab which, by the time it turned in toward the police station, was met by a crowd numbering around two hundred people. As a body they ran toward the cab as it stopped inside the police compound all eager to obtain a glimpse of the murderer. Superintendent Haynes, who had taken charge of the case, moved swiftly to hurry his prisoner through the large steel gates marking the entrance of the station before the crowd had chance to reach them. Such was the local interest generated by the killing. Though there was little to excite those that listened to the evidence produce inside the small court, there was no disputing William Felton had committed murder. Too many witnesses saw the killing in the bar of the Club for there to be any question as to his guilt. What was at stake was whether or not it could be said he was too drunk to know his own actions. No one believed that to be the case; 'wilful murder' was therefore the only verdict the court could bring.

On Friday, 3 February Tom Tingle was laid to rest in West Melton. An hour before the funeral cortège wound it's way along the High Street large crowds had begun to build. By the time it reached the church gates this crowd had spilled over into the churchyard and police were keeping it away from the graveside. So intent were people on showing their feelings toward the murdered man and his family, businesses closed and curtains were drawn across the town as a mark of respect.

Whether Willie Felton had shown any remorse for the killing during the intervening days is not known, but over the two days of Monday and Tuesday, 6 and 7 February, at Rotherham Courthouse, his intention to plead on a charge of manslaughter was made evident to the court. He had little choice. The evidence ranged against him was simply overwhelming. Whatever had been in his mind when he walked from the games room of the Wath and Melton WMC into the bar held little sway with the Rotherham Committal hearing. They were only interested in the fact that at 10.50 pm that night he stabbed Tom Tingle to death. Like the inquest, days earlier, *wilful murder* was the only verdict they could return.

The Trial at Leeds Assizes opened on 21 March 1911 before Mr Justice Horridge. The defence from the outset was that Felton had never intended to murder Tom Tingle; that he had been under the influence of alcohol at the time, severely restricting his ability to think in a rational manner. Grievous Bodily Harm and no more, was the intention when he drew the knife that night. There could be no verdict other than that of Manslaughter. There was little choice for the defence counsel, but their argument that Willie Felton had indeed never intended serious harm should come to Tingle was certainly borne out by testimony of witnesses. Those who had given their evidence to the Rotherham court were brought before the Leeds jury. None varied from the original statements they had made. But more credence was given to the evidence they gave in relation to how they viewed Felton's state of mind at the time of the event they witnessed. This in turn, as it was intended to do, led the jury through a series of acts, rather like an audience to a play. Each scene intended to show the irrational manner in which Willie Felton had conducted himself that night. It was, as *The Advertiser* put it, 'a valiant defence'.

Justice Horridge in his summing up to the jury told them they could not agree with the defence argument that Felton had committed Manslaughter unless they were certain that Felton had been so drunk on the night of the killing, he had not known he would inflict so deadly a wound when he struck out:

A blow of this kind constituted murder unless they could reduce it...

They must, he argued, examine the provocation Felton was under at the time he struck out at Tingle and whether or not that provocation had been sufficient to warrant the verdict of murder:

They must weigh, and weigh very carefully, with the full responsibility that rested upon them from saying whether these were not matters most carefully to be considered. It was not the case of a man who had his cap taken off and pulled out his knife there and then and where he pulled it out, stabbed the man there and then. 'No' he said, 'I am going out, when I come back, see if you do it again.' They had to consider whether that did not show that the prisoner knew perfectly well what he was doing, even if he had had a considerable amount of drink. He left the room. Was that the action of a man who was suffering from provocation, or did it indicate that he had made up his mind, and knew perfectly well what he was doing?... The law in England was beneficent in this way. It said the infliction of a deadly wound of this kind which caused death, was an act of murder in the eye of the law; but knowing the frailties of human nature, there had been engrafted on that rule this. That if the provocation given is, in the opinion of the judge, legal provocation, the jury may, if they are satisfied that the provocation was of such a character that it, in fact, created a state of mind in the prisoners brain that caused the act, then they might reduce it to manslaughter... .

The jury retired at 3.30 in the afternoon. It took only thirty minutes to find Willie Felton guilty of murder, though they did recommend mercy. For Mr Justice Horridge there was only one sentence. Placing the black cap upon his head he agreed with the juries verdict and sentenced Felton to death.

Within days an appeal had been launched and a petition raised. In West Melton opinion was firm in the belief Felton had acted irrationally when he murdered Tom Tingle. The view was that malice never came into it. Felton, they believed, had never intended to kill when he took the knife from his pocket. So far out of character was he there could be no explanation other than he was too drunk to appreciate his actions. They did not believe he should hang for a moment of irrational behaviour, even though it resulted in the death of another man. Over 800 signed a petition that then found its way across the Pennines to Oldham from where Willie Felton had packed up his family and set out for Rotherham ten years earlier.Here the number of signatories grew to over a thousand.

On 1 April 1911 the Home Office wrote to Mr Gichard, the Rotherham solicitor who had acted in defence of Willie Felton, and informed him that the Secretary of State had decided, after receipt of this petition and reviewing the juries verdict, to commute the sentence to life.

Chapter 9

The Killing of Innocence – Amy and Frances Nicholson 1912

Amy Nicholson was the adopted daughter of Arthur and Sarah Collinson.[8] The illegitimate daughter of Sarah's sister, Hannah, whom they had adopted in 1904 when Amy was two years old. They had two other children, both boys, and had changed the girl's name to Collinson in order to avoid gossip. The family moved from Wroot, near Doncaster in January 1912 to take over the tenancy of Abdy Farm, Kimberworth Park. Whilst some half a mile away, at Scholes Coppice, brother in law, Isaac Nicholson and his wife Dora, had taken a cottage in the shadow of Keppel's column at around the same time. The Nicholson's seven-year-old daughter, Frances, was Amy's constant companion and firm friend.

Redscope School, the site of Abdy Farm. The Author

Binder's Farm before it was demolished in the 1950s. Mr R Newton

Both girls attended Meadowhall School and on 15 November 1912 they were to take part in a rehearsal for the school's Christmas concert to be held inside the Old Chapel at Kimberworth village. Both girls were highly excited at the prospect of being a part of the school pageant and wanted desperately to attend, not so the parents. This was to be the first rehearsal held at night. The streets would be unlit when the children left the hall and Frances was afraid of the dark. Despite the excitement generated by the girls throughout the days leading up to the rehearsal and Frances' assurance she would be all right if she stayed with Amy, both sets of parents had serious misgivings. Compromise was reached when Dora Nicholson agreed to her daughter returning from school to Abdy Farm and setting out for the rehearsal from there rather than from Scholes alone. Isaac Nicholson then agreed to send Frances' two brothers to the farm later that same night to collect her and walk her back home. It seemed the perfect solution.

Abdy Farm lay three hundred yards west of Binder's Farm, both occupying adjacent land on Kimberworth Road, now Redscope School. Behind both farms the land was partly cultivated, separated by a hedgerow with a large open spring lying just beyond Abdy Farm's outbuildings. The safest way to walk toward Kimberworth village at night was to leave by the front of the farm, pass Binder's (now the site of *The Dominoe* public house), turn right

Keppel's Column. Scholes Coppice once lay behind and below. The Author

along a track that ran to the Toll Bar House which straddled Wortley Road, then walk along Old Wortley Road until you reached Kimberworth village. As Sarah Collinson gave the girls their evening meal that night, this was the route she instilled in their minds. There was no argument from either, they knew the path well and recognised it's importance. Still excited and eager to be off they set out at a little after half past five that evening.

By 6 pm the girls were safely inside the hall and reciting the poetry they had spent a week learning and by around 7.30 pm they were playing outside Mr Morton's shop, near to the junctions of Kimberworth and Meadowhall Road. They stayed there until 8.00 pm when the group they were with began to break up. Amy, Frances, Doris Wood, Emily Stainrod and Ivy Broomhead drifted off toward the *Sir Colin Campbell* pub. Here they stayed, outside Emily Stainrod's house,[9] until around 8.50 pm when Doris Stainrod came out to call her younger sister in. At this point Amy became a little agitated at having to walk home in the dark and complained of being hungry. Doris took

Kimberworth Old Chapel Hall, where the two girls attended the school Christmas concert on the night they were murdered. Mr R Corker

Sir Colin Campbell *public house, outside which the girls played before setting off home*. The Author

The Effingham Arms *public house. The stone cottages in which Doris Wood and Ivy Broomhead once lived stood to the right of the pub*. The Author

the little group indoors and her mother gave them all a slice of bread and butter and tea.

Amy, Frances, Doris Wood and Ivy Broomhead then left the Stainrod's at around 9 pm and set out on the short walk to the Toll Bar House. It would take them no more than ten minutes to reach the only lighted area they would meet before they arrived back at Abdy Farm. Once there they crossed the road and made for the gate that would lead them onto the footpath home. As they reached the stile beside this gate, a man, clearly drunk, emerged from the shadows. Annoyed at having to move he became abusive and swore at them. Amy and Frances, clearly scared of the man, quickly climbed the stile and ran off into the darkness. Doris Wood and Ivy Broomhead then went off along Upper Wortley Road to their homes near the *Effingham Arms* pub opposite Droppingwell Road.

Back at Abdy Farm Sarah Collinson had started to become concerned at around 8.30 pm that night. This had been the pre-arranged time by which they were to have been back at the farm. The two Nicholson boys had been at the farm waiting for their sister since 7 pm. So trimming a lantern, she sent William, the elder of the two, along with her son Arthur out along the footpath to find the girls and bring them home. They were back forty-five minutes later empty handed. After some discussion with her husband, it was decided to send both of the Nicholson boys back out, but this time once they reached the Toll Bar House they were to set out for Droppingwell and the row of stone cottages where Ivy Broomhead lived. From there they could send Amy home and continue on to Scholes with Frances. Nothing more was heard until half past ten that night when Isaac Nicholson turned up at the farm to say his sons had arrived back and had not found the girls.

Arthur Collinson, trimmed another lantern and the two men set out for Binder's Farm to check whether or not Henry Binder's children had seen Amy or Frances at the church hall. Drawing a blank they left the farm after a few fruitless minutes and were met by PC Thorpe as they walked back out onto Kimberworth Park Road. After listening to their concerns he agreed to join their search and the three set out for Kimberworth. By 3 am the search area had been widened and the searching group joined by concerned neighbours and an ever increasing number of policemen. At some point around four o'clock in the morning, having found no trace of either girl it was decided to call off the search until daylight. They resumed at a little after 7 am.

Dora Nicholson arrived at Abdy Farm that morning just after this second search had begun. She wanted Sarah to join her and meet up with Isaac in Kimberworth. But Sarah, who

The pathway the girls were meant to use on the night they were murdered. The Author

had her own young children to worry about, said she could not leave them alone so would stay at the farm and await news. She told Dora to walk across the fields at the back of the farm because it was the quickest way to reach the Toll Bar house and Kimberworth. Sarah said she would walk with her as far as the spring. As the two reached the water Dora noticed a hat lying beneath the hedgerow off to her right. Recognising immediately that it belonged to Amy she and Sarah ran over to investigate further. As they reached the hedge they could clearly see the two girls laying side by side and believed them to be asleep. It took a moment before they realised the girls were dead. Their throats had been cut.

Dr Alfred Robinson, Borough Medical Officer, examined the bodies at half past nine that morning and determined the girls had been dead for about twelve hours. The bodies lay approximately 120 yards from the back door of Abdy Farm, were clearly overlooked by the upper windows of the farm and appeared not to have struggled with their killer. Detective Inspector Altoft took initial charge of the police investigation. It was his careful examination of the crime scene that set the criteria for the coming investigation.

Around the area where both bodies had been found clear imprints of corduroy fabric were found indicating that the killer had knelt beside the two girls before crawling through a gap found in the hedgerow. In a similar location were imprints made by boots with steel toecaps and hanging from the hedge just above the bodies a man's woollen glove, size six. There was sufficient blood found on the girls and on the ground to suggest the girls had been murdered where they lay. No serious attempt had been made to hide them though some undergrowth had been thrown over them.

By mid morning, because of the developing high profile of the case, Detective Inspector Altoft handed over responsibility for the investigation to Rotherham's Chief Constable, Edwin Weatherhogg.[10] He in turn had the site covered over to protect it from the encroaching weather and had a bloodhound brought to Rotherham from Sunderland. The dog arrived at 11 pm that night and the first serious search began to find the killer. After an arduous trek across open countryside the group of police officers following in the dog's wake were led from Kimberworth Park to Bradgate and then on toward Greasbrough, where the scent was finally lost. Undeterred, a second dog was brought in from Leeds and the search resumed early the following morning. Similar story, similar location but no conclusion. The idea of using dogs was then abandoned.

Meantime Dr Alfred Robinson had concluded his post-mortem examination of the two young girls. He was able to show both had been attacked by a knife which severed the jugular and the wind pipe, death would have been instantaneous. Furthermore, Frances had bruising to her chest which suggested the murderer had knelt on her to carry out the killing. Important because it showed the killer probably took significant bloodstaining. He was also able to show that Amy had been raped, not on the night she was murdered but probably two or three days earlier.

This last piece of evidence was damning and would change the police's initial killer profile. Rape, carried out days earlier, meant Amy quite possibly knew her killer. That her murder was possibly carried out in order that the rapist could maintain his anonymity. Within forty-eight hours police opinion was hardening that the killer was a local man, obviously known to Amy and in all probability to them both. The killer, they hypothesised, was a man with whom they felt safe. A man who had either met the girls as they came onto the footpath and walked across the field with them or a man who met them as they emerged from the darkness at the back of the farm. The lack of any significant struggle and the fact both were found side by side, suggested strongly they were not afraid of the man they met. No attempt appeared to have been made to run away, no shouts or screams were heard, yet they were almost at the backdoor of the farm house and safe. Unfortunately for Arthur Collinson suspicion fell upon him. He fit the profile police had put together and they began to believe he had both motive and opportunity. There was a developing view that he could have met them that night. He, so the argument ran, knew the layout of the land, where exactly the girls would be if they came across the back field and where the best place would be to carry out a murder.

The murdered girls' grave, by A Clark. Rotherham Library Archive

As the investigation continued the funeral of the two little girls took place on 20 November at the parish church, Kimberworth. The coffins were carried from their respective homes and at the junction of Oaks Lane and Wortley Road the two funeral cortège's met to form one long silent procession. From here it wound its way slowly into Kimberworth village. The route lined by thousands who had travelled from outlying area's and villages and as the coffins passed, the crowd fell in behind until, as it reached the church, their number had swollen to over fifteen thousand. If ever a public display demanded justice for the two girls this was it.

The inquest took place on 26 November at the Borough Court House before Coroner Mr W J Bradford and Chief Constable Edwin Weatherhogg, evidence being taken from all parties, particularly the Collinson's who were recalled to the stand after the post mortem detail had been given. The evidence of rape against Amy was both graphic and brutal. The court spent a deal of time attempting to show just when this rape could have taken place. Medical evidence given by Dr Alfred Robinson, surgeon to the Rotherham County Borough police, whilst being precise as to the nature of the injuries sustained by Amy as a result of this rape, was less than precise in judging just when it had taken place:

Chief Constable:	*Would you go so far as to say the girl Amy had not been outraged that night?*
Dr Robinson:	*My opinion is she was not outraged that night, but I would not go as far as to swear definitely.*
Chief Constable:	*Might it have taken place a few hours before?*
Dr Robinson:	*It might, but my opinion is that it was some time previous.*
The Coroner:	*When you say some time you mean days at least?*
Dr Robinson:	*Yes.*

In recalling Sarah Collinson the Coroner's intent was to try and illicit a little more detail as to just when this sexual assault had taken place. He questioned her at length about whether or not Amy had complained of being molested or approached by a man. Sarah was adamant, Amy had never mentioned any such thing. So he began to question her about the underclothes she wore and how often they were changed. Dr Robinson in earlier evidence to the court had stated he found blood staining her drawers and chemise. The coroner wanted to know if Sarah Collinson had been aware. She told him she had not and that the clothes in question had been put on clean on the Monday prior to her murder. So at the very least the Coroner was able to show that the rape had taken place during the week before her death and in all probability during one of the first four days of that week.

By 30 November this had made no difference to the enquiry. Arthur Collinson's possible involvement was being taken less seriously, his movements on the night of the killings substantiated and no evidence found that would in any way implicate him in any aspect of the enquiry. It was decided to hand over the case to Scotland Yard. But by this late stage in the investigation most leads had been exhausted and the involvement of the London force did little to uncover others. As Christmas approached the investigation had started to grind to a halt. It was looking increasingly likely no arrest would ever be made and the crime would simply slip quietly into the unsolved files. Then on 29 December unemployed labourer, Walter Sykes, during a discussion in a public toilet with a man named Vesey Hague, admitted to the murder. Hague wanted the £100 reward which had been put up at the end of November and wasted no time in calling the police. Sykes was duly arrested and in an interview with Police Inspector Barraclough reiterated his confession:

Well I may as well tell the truth, it is the first time I have mentioned it to anybody since I did it. The murder at Rotherham. I did it with a penknife with two blades. I was the worse for drink at the time. I have sold the knife since. I am wearing the same clothes now except the trousers, which were worn out. I slept out that night, and I went to Hemsworth next day.

One hour later he retracted this statement then, when reinterviewed at 7 pm that same night, reaffirmed his involvement. The statement itself was less than explicit. It offered no explanation as to why? Nor did it furnish police with detail as to when? Despite requests for more information Sykes was never able to provide any. So police began a search to locate the necessary evidence to give credence to the confession he had made. First the discarded trousers. These were easy to find. At no time did Walter Sykes refuse to help where he knew he could. The trousers, he explained, had been discarded on Hemsworth Common because he had been given new ones by the Hemsworth Workhouse. In the case of the knife Sykes told police he had sold it for tuppence to a man living in lodgings somewhere in Rotherham, but he did not know the man's name. By early January Herbert Hardy had come forward as that man and produced the knife he had bought from Sykes whilst in a pub. But it had only a single blade not the double blade Sykes had talked of in his statement. Yet Sykes was adamant this was the only knife he had ever owned so police took the view he had simply been mistaken in his recollection of it's ownership.

Within days further evidence came through, eye witnesses who claimed they had seen Sykes either during the week of the murder, outside the church hall on the night of the murder or in the vicinity of the crime scene on the day the bodies were found. The case against him was beginning to build with alarming speed. On 4 January, probably frightened by the events he had set in motion, Walter Sykes retracted his statement for the second time and proclaimed his innocence. It made little difference to the ongoing enquiry.

At 10 am on the morning of 21 January he stood in the dock of Rotherham courthouse still pleading his innocence and listened intently as police rolled out the case against him. He was unrepresented and most probably in awe of his surroundings. Mr Harold Pearce, who undertook the case for the crown opened proceedings with one simple fact. Sykes had confessed. The retraction, he argued, held little weight. If Walter Sykes had not killed the two little girls then he had to explain his movements on the night the murders took place. The confession would stand against him if he could not prove to police officers he had lied and offer up corroborating evidence to support his retraction. Of course Walter Sykes could not do that. In the seventeen days since his change of mind he had failed miserably to find any witness able to substantiate his amended version of events. In fact he had been unable to offer up any account of his movements that did not, after investigation, prove groundless.

Nothing produced in court that day condemned him. Forensic evidence carried out on both the knife and his trousers found no signs of blood. Dr Robinson, who examined the bodies at the scene and had later conducted the post mortem, was unable to confirm the knife recovered by police was the weapon used in the killings. Eye witness accounts from people claiming to have seen Walter Sykes in the crucial days before and after the murder were found to be at odds with those of his employer. William Gedney, who owned a number a fairground rides, had employed Sykes during November. There were no wages paid, just food and lodgings. In turn this meant Gedney had a reasonably good idea of just where his employee had been on most days of the week. The account he gave of Walter Sykes movements through the days leading up to the killings, corroborated by his wife, allowed little chance that he could have been seen by those who claimed otherwise. Samples of corduroy produced in court as possibly having been used by Sykes to repair the knees of his trousers did not conclusively match the imprints found in the ground at the crime scene. Neither did the trousers produced in court as having been those worn by Sykes on the night of the killings have any corduroy patches on them. Finally, the landlady with whom Sykes had been lodging throughout that week in November, told the court he had arrived at her lodging house in Darfield, at 10 am on the morning the bodies were found. He had no bloodstaining on his clothing and told her he had been delivering a horse and dray for a man called Tommy Sopps which had taken him most of the night. Tommy Sopps of course denied any such thing. Sykes was sent for trial at Leeds Assizes.

On 10 March 1913 Sykes again stood in the dock, this time he was fighting for his life. The evidence produced in Rotherham was re-stated as was his retracted confession. Omitted from the case, as it had been in Rotherham, was any reference to the rape of Amy. There was no evidence to support the idea that Sykes had raped the girl two or three days earlier in the week of her death or that her ensured silence had been a motive for her murder. Police had decided to simply accept Sykes' premise that the killing was opportunist, no more no less. As the trial closed Walter Sykes took the stand in his own defence. If he had certain knowledge of his movements on the night the two girls were murdered then this was his opportunity to tell the world. He failed miserably. All he was able to say in his defence was that he had spent the night at his lodgings. This, in spite of his own landlady having told the court he had not returned home that night, he insisted to be true. The prosecution refused to continue with any serious cross examination at that point. Sykes, they argued had told a variety of untruths, this last untruth being so ridiculous as to warrant no further time being spent by them in challenging what was so blatant a lie.

The Jury took eight minutes to accept his guilt and he was duly sentenced to death on 1 April 1913. An appeal lodged shortly after the verdict passed the case to the Home Office and the execution date was postponed. Sykes however was not to be reprieved and on 23 April he was hung at Wakefield Gaol.

Chapter 10

A Lovers Tiff –
Murder and Suicide
1913

Twenty-nine-year-old Laura Gibson lived with her invalid mother Violet Watkin at The Green, West Melton. Apart from a disastrous three-month marriage she had lived her whole life there. In early 1912 she struck up a relationship with George Roebuck, an impressionable eighteen-year-old coal miner. The relationship blossomed, so much so that George became besotted by Laura and on New Year's day 1913 he left his parents house on Hoober Hill to move in with Laura and her mother.

Violet Watkin was unhappy from the outset with the arrangement as were George's parents. Whilst Laura had taken men home before, George was young, inexperienced and could at times be difficult. For a woman partially paralysed it complicated life more than she would have wished. But Laura had her way and as summer came to an end the two were sharing a bedroom. The only consolation for Violet was the money George paid each week toward his upkeep. For a while life was reasonably calm but as the days shortened and winter set in the relationship began to cool. George was a jealous man, constantly seeking reassurance from Laura that she was faithful, that there were no other interests in her life. Laura in turn had begun to tire of having to account for every moment of her life and inevitably the two began to argue. Violet decided George had to go. In October she took in a lodger, George Smith, who paid rent sufficient to replace that lost should George be forced out. She could see no further reason for him to stay and had told Laura he ought to leave.

On Saturday, 15 November 1913 Kate Thornley, Laura's aunt, arrived at the house intending to spend a few days with her sister. George was less than happy at the prospect and spent much of the day drinking. At some point during that Saturday evening he returned home somewhat the worse for wear. Violet, unhappy at the state he was in, gave vent to her feelings and an argument ensued. During this argument the subject of him being allowed to continue to live at West Melton was raised. Violet was adamant he had to go and the argument raged on until the early hours of Sunday morning. At some point Laura agreed with her mother which angered George to such an extent he packed his clothes in a bag and stormed out of the house. Menacingly, before he left, he threatened to return and kill them both. Neither took the threat seriously.

George resentful and angry went straight back to his parents house at Hoober Hill but returned to West Melton at ten o'clock Sunday morning to collect the rest of his things. He only stayed a few minutes and the atmosphere was somewhat strained. Laura made no attempt to reconcile their differences prefering instead to stay out the way until he left.

On Monday, 17 November she and her aunt Kate spent the day in Barnsley where they both had friends. They returned to West Melton at a little after half past ten that night, with Laura in good spirits. After sharing a light supper she wanted to go to bed. It had been a difficult few days and she was tired. Asking her mother for two matches she went out of the back door intending to walk across the yard to the outside toilet. Some ten minutes later she staggered back into the house clutching her throat, blood spouting from an open wound and fell onto the rug in front of the fire. Violet screamed for the lodger George Smith who had been outside at the opposite end of the yard shovelling coal into a bucket. When he got into the house Laura was kneeling up, her hands held out in front of her, with blood pouring from an open wound in her neck. Leaving her, he ran to fetch Dr Gray the local GP whilst Kate Thornley tried to hold Laura upright. Desperate to know who had attacked her both women were shouting questions at her, but it became quickly apparent that she was unable to speak. The wound across her throat had severed the vocal cords as well as her wind pipe. So Violet asked her to nod her head if she had been attacked by George Roebuck, Laura nodded affirmatively.

Map of Elsecar, 1913.
Ordnance Survey, Rotherham Archives
and Local Studies Library

There was nothing that could be done to save Laura's life. When Dr Gray arrived he knew the extent of her injuries were such that death was inevitable. Obviously he did what he could but she died at a little after 1 am in the morning. Being unable throughout the remaining hour or so of her life to tell either him or the police, who had also arrived at the house, anything of value. All anyone knew at that juncture was based upon a series of affirmative nods of the head given by the dying woman in answer to questions put to her by both her mother and her aunt.

By 2 am, police were at Roebuck's parents house. George was not there and had not returned home since leaving at around 7 pm. They carried out a search of all the rooms in the house in an attempt to uncover anything that would tell them where he may have gone that night. No clothes were found to be missing, neither were any of the personal belongings he had brought back with him from West Melton on the Sunday morning. Disturbingly, Thomas Wilburn, George's brother in law, who, because he had married George's elder sister also lived at the house, told police one of his cut throat razors was missing. Damning enough to support the notion George had been responsible for, what by this time had become murder.

The road to Hoober Stand. Hoober Hill lay just beyond the tree line. The Author

Birks Bridge, as it looks today. The Author

At 5 am on Tuesday, 18 November Fred Taylor, a trammer living in Elsecar, found a pile of clothing neatly folded and placed beside Birks Bridge above the canal. Fred, along with four or five other men, struck a match and knelt down to see what they were. On top of the small pile lay a cap, atop of which was a card with the name, 'G.Roebuck. Hoober Hill'. The men fetched police constable Walter Shawforth. He in turn separated the clothing, a jacket and a waistcoat, then went through each of the pockets in turn. Only the jacket held anything of interest, a bloodstained razor inside its case.

Realising of course he had a suicide he went down to the canal side where, at 6.30 am he discovered the body of George Roebuck. Except for the jacket and waistcoat the body was fully dressed and the hands were inside the trouser pockets. George Roebuck had simply walked into the water and allowed himself to drown.

The inquest into the murder and suicide was held at Wath Town Hall on 19 and 20 November presided over by the Coroner, Mr Kenyon Parker. Dr Gray gave a more detailed

The section of the canal where George Roebuck drowned himself. The Author

account of the wounds suffered by Laura Gibson. The testimony, as horrific as it was graphic, he had no doubt she had been attacked from the front. This was supported by the fact that both of Laura's hands had sustained defensive injuries consistent with having been facing the attacker. In his opinion she would have stood little chance in such a scenario.

In the case of George Roebuck there was little doubt he had been the attacker. The blood found on the razor was human, the science of serology was not available in 1913, so the conclusion drawn was that it belonged to Laura Gibson. The fact he had committed suicide in such a manner also added credence to the idea he had been the murderer. Satisfied as to the evidence made available the jury returned a verdict of murder in the case of Laura Gibson, with regard to George Roebuck, Coroner Mr Kenyon Parker told them :

He had always held the opinion that when a person committed a crime and took his own life to avoid the results of it. It was clearly a case of felo de se. *This was not a case of drowning whilst insane. He had clearly taken his life in order to avoid the consequences of his wicked crime.*

The jury agreed.

Chapter 11

A Case of Unrequited Love –
Mary Ives
1917

In June 1916 Mary Ives was happily married and believed by many to have achieved an enviable life. Husband John was the Sub Postmaster of Wombwell and the business was thriving. There was no reason to suspect their relationship to have been anything other than both fulfilling and successful. But when twenty-six-year-old William Ward walked into the shop at the beginning of July those beliefs were to be severely tested.

Ward, a steel worker by trade, was besotted by the woman behind the counter. So much so that he began to call at the shop on a daily basis. Flattered by the attention Mary fell for his easy manner and gentle charm. Within weeks of him first entering the Post Office she was secretly meeting with him and by August had run away to live with him in Doncaster. But William Ward hid a secret she was never to discover.

There was a flaw in his character and the flaw was jealousy. This key factor in his make up caused him to become insanely jealous of the women in his life. Four years earlier this had almost had catastrophic consequences. Having formed a similar relationship with a bar maid, set up home, moved in and to all intents and purposes been very happy. The flaw in his character took over and in the early part of 1913, without apparent provocation he attacked and tried to kill the woman he then lived with. For that he was tried at Leeds Assizes in September of the same year, convicted and sentenced to twelve months in prison. It was not something he intended anyone to ever know.

For most of 1916 he and Mary Ives lived together in comparative bliss. She obtained a job working in munitions, the First World War was in its second year, shells were in high

Bawtry Road, Brinsworth, 1930-1940. Rotherham Archives and Local Studies Library

demand and women were being drafted into the factories to make them. Ward moved between jobs in various steel works. Work was plentiful and wages good. Then at some point in early 1917 things began to go wrong. For whatever reason Mary became dissatisfied with the way their relationship was developing and left the home they had set up together. She moved to Jansen Street in Sheffield and changed her job, still munitions but in one of the factories dotted around the city. In order to be near her, Ward moved to Attercliffe Road in early April 1917 and began work as a labourer at Thomas Firth & Sons, Tinsley.[11] By May 1917 Mary had begun to set up a new life and had re-established contact with her husband in Wombwell spending the weekend of the 12th there. On Thursday, 17 May William Ward, for whatever reason, paid her a visit at her digs and the two went walking along Bawtry Road toward Brinsworth, it was about one o'clock in the afternoon. At half past three that same afternoon, Harold Wright, a Tinsley blacksmith, saw a brown paper parcel laying in a field belonging to Yew Tree Farm at Brinsworth. Curious at why it should have been discarded and eager to retrieve it lest it be of use he left the footpath he was using to cross the fields and walked the two hundred yards or so toward where it lay. As he reached it he could see, lying beneath the hedgerow were two bodies.

Mary Ives lay face down, her head beneath the hedge her throat cut open and clearly dead. Beside her and to her right, the body of William Ward, his left hand around her waist, his right hand outstretched clutching an open bloodstained razor. He too lay with his head beneath the hedge, his throat cut and again clearly dead. Harold Wright left them where they lay and ran for the police. Detective William Shaw was first on the scene and found nothing to indicate any struggle. The parcel Harold Wright had intended to retrieve contained a hard felt hat, the case fitting the razor held in Ward's hand was found in his pocket along with 12s 11d (65p). There were also a number of letters in Mary's handwritting found in Ward's jacket pocket.

The bodies were moved to *The Atlas* hotel later that day. At 10.30 pm police arrived at the little Sub-Post Office in Wombwell to tell John Ives of his wife's death. What they omitted to tell him at that juncture was that she had been murdered. The circumstances surrounding her death he remained blissfully unaware of until his arrival in Rotherham at half past nine the next morning. Identification he made from her jewellery and the colour of her hair. At the inquest, which opened on Saturday, 19 May, before District Coroner Kenyon-Parker at the same hotel, he was asked if he believed her to have killed herself or to have been murdered. He had no hesitation in telling the court it was opinion William Ward had killed her. He added that whilst he had never met the man he had heard talk of his past which he now knew to be true. Murder, he believed, lay well within his capabilities and when he had last met his wife she had told him that Ward had already threatened her life.

Walter Bird, Ward's brother in law, added to this conjecture and the courts knowledge concerning the man's previous conviction. Furthermore, according to his statement the only reason William Ward had met with Mary on the Thursday was because of an injury he had received at work. Incapacitated

The Atlas *hotel where the inquest on Mary Ives and William Ward was held.* The Author

because of a finger which he had trapped in machinery, he was unable to work until it healed. This in turn had created an opportunity. He had wanted to talk to Mary, possibly try to patch up their differences, so taking advantage of this enforced absence from Thos Firth's he arranged the meeting on Bawtry Road. Why Mary had agreed to it when her life had already been threatened would never be known.

Coroner, Kenyon-Parker, because of both deaths, was keen to know if throughout his association with his brother in law, Walter Bird had ever seen Ward exhibit suicidal tendencies. He said he had not. But Ward, according to Kenyon-Parker who obviously had access to prison records, had certainly exhibited them in the past. He told the court that in 1914 he had attempted to kill himself whilst in prison. No doubt he never revealed that moment of madness to his family but it certainly added credence to the police supposition that Ward had possibly always hidden a darker side to his character. A side that would surface only when he felt his emotional security to be under threat and once in the open would lead inevitably to violence.

Detective William Shaw had made a thorough search of Ward's lodgings and in a tin box, produced in court, had found a number of letters. These were not love letters, though some had been written by Mary Ives, but letters of a very different nature. Several had been written by Mary's husband John in an attempt to wrest her away from a man he considered contemptible. Extracts read to the Coroner also confirmed John Ives had been aware of the threat Ward posed toward Mary. In a letter Ives had written on 20 April 1917 he had said as much when he put into words the fear he believed Mary to be living under.

There was no discussion as to whether or not these letters had a detrimental effect upon William Ward or indeed, whether or not he had ever threatened Mary at any stage of their relationship. All the evidence to that effect was purely circumstantial and Coroner Kenyon-Parker knew this. He knew also there was no evidence to refute such a belief, neither was there any evidence of a third party being involved in the deaths of the two people who still lay in the next room of the *The Atlas* hotel. In agreement with the police case he therefore decided Mary Ives to have been murdered by William Ward who in turn committed suicide.

Chapter 12

The Starving to Death of Little Nellie Gibbins 1918

Walter Gibbins had lived in or around the village of Dragonby in North Lincolnshire for most of his life. Born in 1875, he had married in his mid-twenties and by 1914 had eight children. During that same year one of the children was taken ill and his wife looked to a friend of the family, Rose Proctor, to help nurse the child back to health.[12] Rose, a married women herself with seven children lived nearby and was only too pleased to help. During the course of what proved a long convalescence she and Walter Gibbins became lovers. By the early part of 1915 he had ousted his wife, who went to live at nearby Barton upon Humber, and along with his eight children, moved to Hall Road in Maltby near Rotherham. Rose Proctor with one of her children joined him once he had found work and together they set up home. Over the next two years Rose gave birth to two more children swelling the family total to eleven.

But things were far from happy in the Gibbins household. Rose had proved difficult to live with and resentment at being forced to leave six of her own children back in Lincolnshire began to surface early in the relationship. Almost from day one she showed an indifference toward Walter's children that she did not show to her own. The one child she had taken to Maltby and the two new babies were well treated receiving more food than the others and better clothing. Her adopted family were, to some extent, left to fend for themselves, but the greatest neglect she reserved for one child in particular.

Nellie Gibbins had been only five years old when her father brought her to Maltby. Nothing in her past suggested she was anything other than a happy, boisterous young girl. Within months of Rose Proctor's arrival, her life had entered a downward spiral. For reasons never fully explained she was to become the focus of serious neglect. Forced to spend her days locked in an upstairs bedroom, her only source of company her three brothers with whom she shared the room each night. She was systematically starved of food. At some stages of her short life the only food she received was that provided by her brothers through begging. The children then having to smuggle the food upstairs to her at night. Walter Gibbins was not unaware of his daughters plight. It is known that sometimes, late at night, Nellie would sneak out of her room and go downstairs to beg him to find her something to eat. He in turn would steal scraps from the kitchen or pantry and take them to the squalid little room that had become her life and would secretly feed her. He, just like Nellie, had grown afraid of Rose. To offer succour to his own daughter openly would release a terror he could not cope with. So, over two years she slowly starved to death.

Nellie Gibbins died on New Year's Eve, 1917. After a hurried consultation between Walter and Rose it was decided he would carry her body to his work at the brickyard and he would bury the body where it would never be found. For a while all was well but they were unaware one of Gibbins young sons had seen the dead Nellie before her body had been removed. He somehow got news to his mother at Barton Upon Humber. She in turn notified both the NSPCC and the police.

On or around 29 January 1918 police visited the house in Hall Road and asked to see the little girl Nellie. Rose Proctor, who was home alone, told the officer Nellie had been given to Walter's brother to look after and if they needed further details to call and see Walter at the brickyard. This they did and were told by Gibbins that the child had been taken to his brother's house at Christmas and left there. For the moment, despite the conflicting stories, they were satisfied. But Walter knew they would be back. The story of his brother had been concocted hurriedly shortly after Nellie's death, to fend off enquiries from neighbours, it was never intended to have been as a cover for the police. At 4.30pm that same day, convinced the child's

General view of Maltby, 1915 by J. Simonton & Sons. Rotherham Archives and Local Studies Library

death would be uncovered Walter Gibbins swallowed prussic acid. Believing he would die he made a statement to the brickyard manager before he was stretchered off to Rotherham hospital in which he admitted that his daughter, Nellie, was buried in the yard outside. He blamed Rose Proctor for her death, accusing her of cruelty. The statement was passed to police and Walter Gibbins, who did not die was arrested at the hospital on the following day, Rose Proctor followed within hours.

Their trial opened at Leeds Town Hall on Monday, 18 March. Gibbins, wracked by pain and unable to either walk or

stand because of the effects of Prussic acid, was placed in a reclining position in the dock. Rose Proctor buried her head in a handkerchief and remained in that position for the duration of the trial. Their defence was simply that Nellie had died, not of neglect but of a wasting desease which could not be diagnosed. Prosecuting counsel produced, at the outset of the trial, a photograph taken of the little girls body after it had been recovered from the brickyard. Fierce legal argument centred around its inclusion as evidence but the judge, Mr Justice Roche, took a view that as evidence it was legitimate if not essential and allowed the jury to view it. It damned the couple almost before the trial had opened:

> *Nothing in the pages of Dickens, not even the description of Dotheboys Hall, or of the workhouse baby-farm, can be said to surpass, in the power of moving human indignation against oppression of helpless childhood.*

This was how the *Rotherham Advertiser* reported the prosecutions opening remarks to a packed courtroom. It seemed very apt as the story of little Nellie was slowly revealed to an attentive jury. Rose Proctor wept as the prosecution told how over a two year period she had conceived a 'mysterious and unaccountable hatred' for a seven year old child. How she had openly spoke of the child as, 'poison'. The squalor of the bedroom in which those two years had been spent was eloquently described, as was the imagined confinement and subsequent starvation.

Walter Gibbins was described to the court as a coward, a man whose behaviour was as inexplicable as it was abhorrent; who had for two years lived in fear of the woman he broke his marriage to be with. Despite defence arguments that throughout his life he had cared for his children, tended their needs and provided for their upbringing; that Nellie Gibbin's tragic life he had been largely unaware of, there was no sympathy in the courtroom on that March day.

At 6.00 pm, after advising the jury they had a choice to make, either a verdict of manslaughter or a verdict of wilful murder, the court adjourned. It took only sixty minutes for

Aerial view of Maltby old village.
Rotherham Archives and Local Studies Library

them to return having found both guilty of murder. Judge, Mr Justice Roche, placed the black cap upon his head and turning to both made only one simple statement:

It is no use my speaking about the enormity of your crime, the verdict of the jury shows what it is.

He then passed sentence of death upon them both.

Chapter 13

A Fight at Kilnhurst –
Patrick Gillespie
1923

The younger members of the Muscroft family, of North Terrace, Kilnhurst and the younger members of the Gillespie family, of South Terrace, Kilnhurst hated each other with a passion. There had been serious ill will between the two for years. This had resulted in arguments between the women and fights between the young men. On 13 October 1923 the antagonism between the two families boiled over into a street fight after Anthony Gillespie had been set upon by two of the Muscroft boys. The fighting was brief, quickly broken up and no one was seriously hurt. But for the Gillespie family it was far from over.

On Saturday, 27 October, some two weeks later, young Alec Gillespie walked into the *Commercial Hotel* at Kilnhurst and

The Commercial Hotel, *no longer a public house.* The Author

began to harangue nineteen-year-old Edwin Muscroft who stood drinking at the other side of the bar. According to the landlord his language was intimidating and his demeanour such that unless he had stepped in there would have been a fight in the tap room. Deciding Alec to be the worse for wear through drink he ordered him out of the pub, policing him to the door and out into the street. Edwin made no attempt to follow and stayed drinking with a man named Wilkinson. The two eventually left at a little after 10.00 pm. Walking together along Glasshouse Street they were joined by Harold Dawson and Edwin's sister Ellen Gilliver who had been shopping that night in Mexborough. Within minutes the group were met by the elder of the two Gillespie boys, Anthony, still smarting from his beating two weeks earlier and believing Edwin to have caused his younger brother Alec's eviction from the pub earlier. He wasted no time in striking out at Edwin but, just as it had been two weeks earlier, he found himself hopelessly out-numbered and after a brief scuffle forced to extricate himself. But not before Edwin's sister had run off home to fetch her father.

Fifty-six-year-old Jim Muscroft was less than keen to be drawn into a fight, particularly in the street, only his daughters insistence that he support his son forced him away from his fireside. It was about a 10.15 pm. As he stepped out of the door of his house on North Terrace, no more than a hundred yards ahead of him he could clearly see Anthony Gillespie hiding behind a wall. So, as he stated later, it was clear, any fighting there had been was clearly over and his son in no danger. But having been roused from the house he had no intention of returning until it was clear just what had taken place. He and his daughter met with his son and Harold Dawson as they stood outside the *Nag's Head* public house talking to the landlord, Thomas Thorpe.

Just as this meeting was taking place, fifty-five-year-old Patrick Gillespie was hearing of the trouble his two sons had been in over the previous hour or so. Alec had returned home but not so Anthony. Concerned for his safety and buoyed by alcohol, he went out on to the street to try and find him. He did not have far to go. As he approached the *Nag's Head* it was clear, despite the poor lighting, that the head of the Muscroft

Glasshouse Road as it is today. The terraced housing that once ran alongside the road has long since been demolished. The Author

family was one of a group gathered about the only street light. Believing them to have harmed his son he had no hesitation in walking straight at them. Ellen Gilliver, as she saw the familiar figure loom out of the darkness, stepped out from their midst and with one blow from her right fist felled him. It was a second or two before he regained sufficient composure to pull himself back onto his feet and strike out at Jim Muscroft whereupon confusion reigned. Blows came from all quarters and he was quickly back on the ground. At this point Mary Flannery, Patrick's daughter, came around the corner with her husband William. Both less than sober, they lost no time in attempting to lift Patrick off the ground and drag him away from the group gathering around him. Mary took a blow to the head from Ellen Gilliver which rendered her ineffective but William stoically resisted all attempts to prevent him dragging the now prone Patrick away from the one sided fight. It took two attempts before he was able to get his father in law onto his feet and with the help of a somewhat dazed Mary half carry him back to his house on South Terrace.

After a cursory examination by his wife it was decided his injuries, though not apparently severe, should be seen by a doctor. Mary went to fetch local doctor, Charles Aitken, from his

The site of North and South Terrace. The Nag's Head *public house once stood behind this row of modern housing.* The Author

home on West Street. He stated later that he had found Patrick conscious but sore from a lump at the back of his head, a swollen eye, and a cut face. It was his considered opinion at the time that the injuries were not dangerous. He could not have been more wrong. During the course of the night his condition gradually deteriorated until by early morning he was unconscious and at a little after half past nine that morning he died.

Fifty-six-year-old James Muscroft, nineteen-year-old Edwin Muscroft and twenty-seven-year-old Ellen Gilliver were duly arrested within an hour and charged with having caused the death of Patrick Gillespie. They pleaded their innocence claiming the fight had not been serious enough to have caused the man's death.

The following day all three were arraigned before Mr J S Colton-Fox at the Rotherham West Riding Police Court. Police laid out the evidence of dispute that had taken place between the two families, claiming this to be the sole motive for the killing. Represented by Mr A S Furniss this was immediately refuted. He believed that to accept such a theory was to accept that the defendants were guilty of murder. The charge, he reminded the court, was one of having unlawfully caused death, not the same he argued as having committed murder. It was the courts place to decide which, if any, of the defendants had caused the blow that killed Patrick Gillespie. If that could be proved then murder would be a fair reflection of that truth. Until then he contested, bail should be granted and the charges further investigated:

> Mr Furniss: *It was all right... to say that there*
> *had been violence on both sides,*
> *but it was their contention that the fault*
> *was upon Gillespie's side... magistrates*
> *should not refuse bail unless there were*
> *some very potent and sufficient reasons*
> *for doing so.*

It was not a principle the court entirely agreed with. Magistrates clerk, Mr Clews, took serious issue with the defence argument. To him there could be only one charge in this case:

> Mr Clews: *But this is a charge of murder.*
> Mr Furniss: *This is not a charge of murder.*
> Mr Clews: *You are charged with causing this man's*
> *death, and until the inquest shows how it*
> *was caused, that is murder.*
> Mr Furniss: *Until it is proved that my clients were*
> *directly responsible they should not be*
> *kept in custody. I think that it will be*
> *shown that while it was an exceedingly*
> *unfortunate event for the deceased, it was*
> *caused entirely by his own conduct.*

Mr Colton-Fox was having none of it. He adjourned the proceedings after an hour remanding the three to custody for a further two days. Whether it be murder or otherwise, he argued, the defendants had been seriously involved and, therefore, could not be allowed to move back into the community until the case be resolved.

The inquest opened on Tuesday, 30 October in the Public Library, Swinton before Coroner Mr Kenyon Parker. He instructed the jury that the purpose of the day was to hear evidence of identification and post mortem results only at that juncture, but that they would be expected to return a criminal verdict at the inquests conclusion. The medical evidence when it came was inconclusive as far as the Muscroft family were concerned. Dr S O Hatherley, police surgeon, confirmed that Patrick Gillespie had been beaten, that could be evidenced from the cut to his lip, abrasions to his eyebrow and forehead. He had died as a result of a blow to the back of the head which had caused a fracture of the skull. Whether that blow had come from any of his attackers or as a result of him hitting the pavement was simply not possible to say. The inquest was adjoined at that juncture for a further week.

The following day all three defendants were back at the Rotherham West Riding Police Court. The court this time being presided over by Mr E Rose. As a direct result of the findings of the earlier inquest Mr Furniss, who continued to defend the three, immediately repeated his application for their release on bail. Arguing strongly that no evidence had been presented at the coroner's court that could substantiate murder and that being the case they should not be held in prison. There followed a repeat of the debate that had taken place two days earlier. Prosecuting counsel this time requested more time to collate all the necessary evidence to allow them to bring a possible charge of murder. The court acceded and sent the three back to prison.

The resumed inquest, upon which so much rested, finally took place on Tuesday, 6 November. Key witness to the events that night was David Squires, a man who had been in the Gillespie house just before Patrick left and who also saw the fight unfold as he stood at the bottom of South Terrace and

Parish church of St Thomas, Kilnhurst where Patrick Gillespie is buried. The Author

watched. He had been interviewed by police twenty four hours later and in his statement had said that Edwin Muscroft had kicked Gillespie twice on the head. This, as far as the prosecution were concerned could well have been sufficient to have caused the fractured skull which precipitated Gillespie's death. Yet when he took the stand at the Coroner's court he told a slightly different tale:

> ...*Gilliver* [Ellen] *said a nasty word to Gillespie, who replied 'I won't have anything to do with you.' Then Mrs Gilliver hit Gillespie in the face with her right fist, and knocked him to the ground on the footpath. Gillespie was getting up when Jim Muscroft knocked him down with a blow... Edwin Muscroft kicked Gillespie twice in the stomach. Flannery* [William] *was picking up Gillespie when Edwin knocked him clean out of his arms. Mrs Flannery got hold of Gillespie and received a blow in the face from Gilliver* [Ellen]... .

Furniss, still defending the three, was on the change of story like a shot. He wanted to know why Squires had now decided that the blows to the head he had earlier claimed had been made by Edwin Muscroft were now to the stomach. There was a long moment of silence. The court waited, clearly David Squires had exaggerated his earlier statement and Furniss wanted him to admit as much. Finally, and with some hesitancy, he acknowledged what he termed a mistake, and agreed this latest statement was accurate.

No other witness called to the stand throughout the remainder of the day was able to state categorically that they saw any of the three defendants strike Gillespie at the back of the head. Only Edwin Muscroft, who took the stand at the end of the day's proceedings added further detail. He agreed with David Squires version and told the court he had struck out twice at Gillespie. But in his version of events the second blow knocked Gillespie backward and as he fell his head struck the causeway beneath him.

As the day came to a close Mr Kenyon-Parker conducting the day's proceedings accepted the notion that no single blow had been responsible for Gillespie's death. He told the jury that because of the amount of conflicting evidence, none of which identified the killing blow, it was impossible to state with any certainty that murder had been committed:

> *If you should come to the conclusion that the evidence does not Justify a verdict of* Wilful Murder, *but does justify a verdict of Manslaughter, and should feel a little doubt as to which of these blows or falls actually did the mischief - the fracture of the skull: then do you think it would do harm or good to the village of Kilnhurst, and to those families who seem to have some sort of feud against one another, if you decided all these three persons richly deserved to be sent for trial.*

It took twenty minutes for the jury to accept the premise set by the Coroner and return a 'manslaughter' verdict against all three.

Three hours later, at a special evening session of the Rotherham West Riding Police Court, they were back in court. This time to decide whether or not the Court would uphold the inquest verdict of manslaughter and accept bail. They would not.

Public Prosecutor, Mr Pashley, told the court the inquest had no bearing upon the Police court and it was his intention to proceed with a charge of murder. Outrage followed from a defence who argued strongly that it was inappropriate to talk of murder when a Coroner's court could find nothing to substantiate the charge. Fierce legal debate followed but the charge was upheld. The three defendants, now formally charged with wilful murder were again remanded.

On Wednesday, 14 November the committal proceedings finally got under way. Key witness once more, David Squires. This time he had a revised version of events. Obviously having reconsidered his evidence he had decided that his first statement was the more accurate of the two he had made. He told the court that he had witnessed two kicks to the head not the stomach as he had said at the inquest, claiming confusion and nerves had gotten the better of him eight days earlier. Rigorous cross questioning by the defence, still ably conducted by Mr Furniss, failed to shift him this time. So it fell to Dr Sidney Oldfield Hatherley, the Police Surgeon, who had carried out the post mortem examination, to refute Squire's eye witness evidence, he duly obliged:

Mr Furniss:	*Could the injury on the left side of the eye have been caused by a fist ?*
Dr Hatherley:	*Yes*
Mr Furniss:	*Do you agree that the injury at the back of the head could have been caused by a fall on the kerb ?*
Dr Hatherley:	*Yes. I do not agree with the suggestion that there could have been two kicks on the same spot...*

No further evidence was offered to support the notion of murder but what was forthcoming was evidence supporting the supposition that the Muscroft family, particularly Edwin and his sister Ellen, were known for violence. Police Constable Walker who had been stationed in Kilnhurst since March 1922 knew the warring families well. On the night of Gillespie's death he had visited the dying man at home some half an hour or so after the fight. Whilst in the house he heard shouting coming from a house which backed on to the Gillespie's yard. Leaving Patrick Gillespie to be attended by his doctor, he went to investigate the commotion and found Edwin Muscroft beating the householder, Jack Haythorne. After pulling the two men apart Muscroft left only to return several minutes later with his father Jim, his mother and sister Ellen. Immediately they arrived at the house Edwin began striking out at Haythorne again and only the threat of arrest, met by a verbal tirade from Ellen Gilliver, put a stop to it.

Despite defence arguments that this was no more than a Saturday night quarrel and that the events after the street fight had no relevance to the charge the point had been made. It took twenty minutes for the ruling magistrates to accept there was a *prima facia* for murder and sent the three for trial at Leeds Assizes.

The trial opened on Wednesday, 6 December before Mr Justice Talbot. No new evidence was produced for the jury and the argument remained, as it had been over the previous seven weeks, one of culpability. In his summing up the judge told the jury the prisoners were not guilty of murder but possibly manslaughter. The task he set them was decide if one or all had been a party to Patrick Gillespie's death:

> ...*with regard Edwin Muscroft there was very little contradiction on the essential points. There was undoubtedly more contradiction with regard to James Muscroft, and with regard to the female prisoner there was direct contradiction. On the broad face of the facts. Edwin Muscroft fought Gillespie and that fight resulted in the death of Gillespie.*

It took twenty-five minutes for the jury to find Edwin Muscroft guilty of manslaughter, for which he received a sentence of eighteen months hard labour. The other two were found not guilty and discharged.

Chapter 14

The Secret Affair of Alfred Bostock
1925

Alfred Bostock had been born in Barnsley in 1900 and orphaned at a young age.[13] He and his brother had been brought to live in Rotherham by their uncle and aunt, where they took up residence in a row of terraced cottages near Parkgate. After leaving school he had gone straight to work at Parkgate Steel Works where, in 1916, he first met Elizabeth Sherratt. It was a relationship destined to last only two years and after the break up he left his job to join the army. It was 1918 and the First World War was still raging across Europe. If he had designs on glory he was to be sorely disappointed, being posted to Ireland where he stayed for almost two years, returning to Rotherham in 1920. Within months of this return he was back working as a crane driver at Parkgate Steel Works.

Whether or not he made any attempt at that stage to rekindle his relationship with Elizabeth is not known, but because both lived within a couple of miles of each other, he in Parkgate she in Claypit Lane, Rawmarsh, it is not beyond the realms of possibility. Elizabeth had also, since 1919, been employed at the Electra Picture Palace in Parkgate. So if he never passed her in the street he certainly would have met her when he went to the cinema.

Either way, by 1923 Bostock had struck up a relationship with a young woman named Ethel who he married later that same year, his new bride giving birth to a daughter shortly afterwards. The three of them settled down to life sharing his parents cottage at Parkgate. With regular work and reasonable wages the marriage ought to have proved successful but the indications are things were not as they seemed.

In January 1925 he received a letter from Elizabeth Sherratt asking if he would meet, ostensibly to discuss old times. Whether as a result of some previous meeting or not is uncertain but Bostock readily agreed. What took place at that meeting has never been made public and Bostock insisted there were no other meetings until April 1925. This second meeting he arranged after his mother received an anonymous letter:

> *Dear Mrs Bostock,*
> *Will you tell your son, Alfred, to come up and save further trouble. I should not have bothered you if I had known his address. One who knows.*

Even if his mother did not realise who had sent the letter Alfred Bostock certainly did. Having known Elizabeth Sherratt for nine years he recognised the handwriting and so lost no time in trying to arrange to meet with her. Being married meant this would be a meeting only he knew about. So on 17 April he wrote a short note:

> *Dear Lizzie,*
> *I want to see you on Saturday night at 9 o'clock at the bottom of Corporation Street. That is a little further on from where you get on the car.*

The meeting, for whatever reason, never took place so he wrote a second letter:

> *Dear Lizzie,*
> *Could you possibly be at the bottom of Green Lane on Monday at 7 o'clock? I want to see you, so don't forget. If you cannot come drop a line to Parkgate Iron and Steel Works. It will find me. I would like to see you. So long.*
> *Alf*
>
> *P.S. Bring this letter with you as I have something to show you.*

Again Bostock waited in vain, so he wrote a third letter:

> *Dear Lizzie*
> *I want you to meet me at the bottom of Green Lane at 7.30 pm. on Sunday night, when you arrange to meet me don't forget and go strolling with another friend. I saw you about 8.45 so don't forget. I shall come fields way.*
> *Alf.*

This third and final letter had the desired effect. On Sunday, 3 May 1925 the two met at the corner of the cricket field in Rawmarsh at the pre-arranged time. Elizabeth had planned to catch a tram to Moorgate and meet with a friend, Rose Flint, so she intended the meeting to be brief.

By 10.00 pm she had not returned home and her father, Thomas Sherratt, alerted his sons and he began what proved an unsuccessful search. The following morning, Mary Sherratt, Elizabeth's sister in law walked from her home on Rawmarsh Hill to Claypit Lane and asked to look in Elizabeth's room. There she found a letter at the bottom of a drawer which had been written the previous day and addressed to Rose Flint. It was a letter apologising for not visiting with her on the Sunday and giving as her reason a meeting she was to have that same night with someone she simply called Alf.

Mary Sherratt roused her other sister-in-law, Ada, and the two walked to Bostock's house in Parkgate. There they confronted him and asked him to explain what had taken place when he and Elizabeth had met on the previous night. He agreed the two had met but claimed he left her at the corner of Goosebutt Street, Parkgate, at between half past seven and twenty minutes to eight. Convinced or not the sisters asked him to help in their search. At first he refused but after a little persuasion by Ada's husband, who accompanied the two, he agreed.

It made little difference. At 11.15 am that same morning, whilst this meeting was taking place police had discovered a woman's body in the River Don, about one hundred yards on the Rotherham side of the Don bridge, head and shoulders submerged, feet resting on a mound of soil. She had clearly been beaten to death and blood splattered the foliage around where she lay. The body was taken to Kilnhurst Mortuary.

At 2.00 pm that same day, Alfred Bostock, having been told of the discovery arrived at the mortuary to carry out an identification. Police immediately took him into the small room in which she lay and he had no hesitation in identifying her as Elizabeth Sherratt. But he made the identification with her face being covered over by a cloth. This one factor led to his immediate arrest.

He told police of his meeting the previous night and that after leaving her he had walked to the *Rail Mill Inn*, arriving around 8 pm. He was able to describe the barmaid that served him drinks and claimed he had left the pub to walk to his mother in law's house at 7 Foljambe Street, Rotherham. Waiting for him when he arrived at a little after 9.30 pm, his wife and daughter. The three of them then walked back to Parkgate. Police formally charged him with murder on the following morning, 5 May.

On 20 May 1925 Bostock was arraigned before Rotherham West Riding Magistrates. During the intervening period between arrest and court hearing police had managed to uncover a great deal with regard to the events of the night of the murder though most of it only circumstantial. But more importantly post-mortem examination had revealed Elizabeth Sherratt to have been pregnant and eight months pregnant at that. This they used to great effect at the Rotherham hearing. The contention was simple enough, Bostock had been told back in January of her pregnancy, hence the first letter. He refused to help, hence the anonymous letter to his mother. This second letter stung him into action because he could not afford

The River Don near to where Elizabeth Sherratt was murdered. The Author

Rawmarsh Hill, 1920 by E L Scrivens. Rotherham Archives and Local Studies Library

his wife to discover he had been unfaithful so he wrote requesting a meeting. When that meeting finally took place he walked her to the river side and beat her nine times with a heavy, blunt instrument, threw that into the river then pushed her face down into the water.

A parade of witnesses were brought into the court room who claimed to have seen him with the dead woman on the night she was murdered. None of their evidence conclusive but enough to place him at the scene of the crime. Work colleagues who knew him and knew him reasonably well told in turn of various workplace conversations in which he had discussed this 'other woman'. He had apparently discussed her pregnancy, expressed his concern at being discovered by his wife and two days prior to her death had allegedly said he would kill her. But whilst this was, in the main hearsay evidence, that given by Lillian Prince who worked as a barmaid at the *Rail Mill Inn* was not. She categorically denied having either seen, or served, Alfred Bostock at any stage of the night on which the murder took place. Further despair came in the form of his mother in law, neither she nor his wife Ethel could corroborate the story he had given police as to the time he arrived at Foljambe Street. According to both women he had arrived at around 10.15 pm not 9.30 pm as he claimed. They were able to be precise because Ethel's father had left the house to go to work at 10.00 pm and Bostock was not there at that time.

It was damning stuff. As the day drew to a close the court had identification evidence placing Bostock with Elizabeth Sherratt between 9 pm and 10 pm at night. Failure to corroborate the time he claimed to have arrived at his mother in laws reinforced the view that this evidence was probably accurate. Added to that was the last piece of identification evidence given that day by William Schofield, who lived on Foljambe street and claimed to have met him at 10 pm as he walked from the *George Hotel*. According to his statement when the two met Bostock asked if he were walking back to Foljambe street and offered to accompany him. The fact the two did not go home together had no relevance, what mattered was that William Schofield worked at Parkgate Steelworks and knew Bostock well. There was no hesitation by the court in committing him for trial to Leeds Assizes.

Alfred Bostock wore a navy blue suit and soft collar as he stood in the dock on 25 July 1925 before Mr Justice Finlay. He pleaded not guilty to a charge of murder. Keith Roddis, the Rotherham solicitor who had handled the case since his arrest continued to act for him and passed occasional messages from the dock to his defence barrister, Mr Streatfield. He remained calm throughout and when the judge allowed him to sit he folded his arms and remained in that position for most of the day. At no time did he appear to show any emotion, remaining impassive even as the details of Elizabeth Sherratt's brutal death were given to the jury.

By midday the array of witnesses, whose identification evidence was so vital to the prosecution, had reiterated their various statements and in turn at times, wilted under cross examination as Streatfield attempted to mitigate the damage they could have caused. By afternoon the various letters written both by Elizabeth Sherratt and Alfred Bostock dominated the proceedings. The claim was simple enough.

Bostock had met with her sometime in August 1924, was responsible for her being eight months pregnant and needed a way out of the situation. Murder was the only recourse open to him if he was to avoid exposure. It was a convincing argument, as it had been in Rotherham. There was little the defence could offer by way of rebuttal even if there was little proof to support the notion.

Later in the day Bostock took the stand. There was little that was new in how he described his movements that night until he arrived at the point at which he claimed to have called into the *Rail Mill Inn* at a little after 9 pm on the night of the murder. This, he now maintained, was wrong, that he had simply confused the names of two pubs in his earlier statements and mistaken the *Rail Mill Inn* for the *Forge Inn*. It was to the second of these two pubs that he had walked that night and because they were located so close together he had mistaken the names when he spoke to police But no corroborating evidence was produced by the defence so, to a large extent it fell upon deaf ears.

High Street, Rawmarsh. Rotherham Archives and Local Studies Library

He was closely cross examined with the regard to the letters. These, particularly those in Bostock's own hand, were sent in order to create an opportunity to carry out the murder. Leastways, that was the claim. Bostock did not deny sending them but refused to be coherced into agreeing they were a means to murder. Instead he argued strongly that had Elizabeth Sherratt never sent the anonymous letter to his mother he would never have set up any meeting with her. But it made no difference to the outcome. On the morning of 26 July Mr Justice Finlay, in recognition of the jury's verdict, sentenced him to death.

Immediately an appeal was lodged with the Home Secretary. This was heard on 18 August. Streatfield setting out three points of defence. One that the identification evidence was inaccurate, two that no proof had been produced to show Bostock as the father of Elizabeth's unborn child and finally that the letters had been used not in the chronological order in which they were sent but in an order which suited the prosecution. It failed on all counts. Alfred Bostock received the news impassively. The last meeting with his wife took place on 3 September and he was hung at 9 am the following morning.

Chapter 15

Murder at Hooton Roberts – Kathleen Roodhouse
1926

As July 1926 came to a close, twenty-four-year-old Cecil Roodhouse, ran out of money. The General Strike had reduced his ability to fund his life to such an extent he was beyond being desperate. He had made two applications to the Guardians[14] for financial relief and received scant attention and no help. So, on Saturday 30 July, he decided it was time to take action. Time to reduce the financial burden placed upon his family by those who, as he viewed it, could not, or would not earn a living.

However, the family, as he termed it, was somewhat fragmentary. Since his father's untimely death at Cadeby Main in 1912, lack of money had meant that as children they had been split up and sent to live with relatives who could both care for them and support them. The original intention had been that this would only last until his mother was able to provide for them adequately. But for Cecil Roodhouse it had lasted for most of his life.

Upon leaving school he had worked firstly in a brickyard, where his right hand had been severely damaged by a machine. This was followed by a spell at Cadeby Colliery as a miner then, possibly to better serve his growing need for independence, he went to sea as a fireman aboard a White Star liner. This lasted until November 1925 when, having achieved what he saw as a deal of self-determination, he felt able to return to Rotherham and live an independent life. Deciding stability lay in the mining industry he resumed his role as a miner but this time working out of Kilnhurst Colliery. Unfortunately he had returned at a time of industrial disquiet, particularly in the pits and this independence was short lived, the strike of 1926 destroying any financial savings he had been able to make and forcing him to take shelter once more amongst relatives who could better support him financially. In May 1926 he moved in with his uncle, Francis Barker, at East Dene. His fourteen-year-old brother Edgar already lived around the corner with an aunt, Mary Hill. This left his unemployed sister Kathleen the only child able to live at home with their mother.

Cecil Roodhouse resented this. For Kathleen to live at home but not work to help pay the cost of her keep was likened in his mind to an act of sedition. There had been talk of her going into service, working as a maid. Nothing ever came of it and Kathleen steadfastly refused to find a job. As the weekend dawned Roodhouse, after spending Friday night in a lodging house in Rotherham, returned to his uncle's house for a change of clothing. The clothes were still damp and he was told to wait an hour or so for them to dry. Agitated, he left without them and sent his brother Edgar to collect them an hour later. He pushed the clothing, neatly wrapped in brown paper, underneath his arm and set out on the long walk to Conisbrough and his mother's home. On route he made a detour at Hooton Roberts, entering the woodland known locally as Hooton Cliff Wood. He walked through the wood until he reached a point where the tree line halted and the land fell away toward a corn field. Here he carefully placed the

Hooton Cliffs, the body of Kathleen Roodhouse was found in this area. Rotherham Archives and Local Studies Library

parcel of clothes so they could not be seen. Then, retracing his steps, he found his way back onto the road and continued his journey to Conisbrough, arriving unexpectedly at around lunchtime. Immediately there followed a long discussion between mother and son about Kathleen's lack of employment prospects. At the end of which he told his mother he could find her work at the home of someone he was familiar with if she were interested. Kathleen seemed reluctant but the idea was not dismissed out of hand. According to Eleanor Roodhouse, the mother involved, there was no apparent ill feeling between brother and sister. He suggested his sister go into Rotherham with him and spend a few days at their cousin Minnie Hamstead's house on Fitzwilliam Road. Kathleen readily agreed and quickly put together a parcel of clothing, enough for two or three days. Once ready Roodhouse asked if she would go to the chemist and fetch him two pennyworth of salts of lemon for soldering before they left. Cecil Roodhouse had purchased this before so it was an acceptable request. She agreed, the salts were bought and Mrs Roodhouse placed them in a small blue bottle marked 'Poison'.

The two set out at 6.30 pm that night, Kathleen, excited at the prospect of being away from home for a few days, Eleanor Roodhouse pleased to have the house to herself for a while and Cecil content his plan was falling into place. At around a 7.15 pm they approached Hooton Roberts and Cecil carefully guided Kathleen into the woodland he had visited some five hours earlier. Reaching the spot where he had hidden his clothes he dropped back and fell in behind his sister. She never saw the blow that struck her at the back of the head. Stunned, she fell to her knees and Roodhouse pushed her onto her back. Realising what was about to happen she began to scream. He quickly placed his hands about her throat and squeezed until she stopped struggling. Once dead he rolled her body into the undergrowth, covered her over, then sat back on the grass and swallowed the contents of the bottle of salts he had her purchase before they began their journey. Salts of Lemon was a common name for hydrochloric acid. It had been his intention from the outset to commit suicide once he had murdered his sister. Unfortunately the liquid merely made him vomit and had no lasting effect. Retrieving the clothing he had hidden earlier he changed. Using the same brown paper he then parcelled up his discarded clothes and took that, along with the parcel his sister had carried, and set off for the Rotherham Road. At some point in the wood he threw her parcel into a stream, his own he discarded in a ditch beside a cultivated field known as Hooton Field. Ellen Parkin, who lived in Hooton Roberts, saw him do it and the parcel was recovered by her husband. It was 7.30 pm at night and Kathleen Roodhouse had only left the safety of her mother's house one hour earlier. She was seventeen years old.

At a little after 8 pm, sore from the acid he had swallowed, he made his way to Holland's farm just beyond the woodland in which Kathleen lay. He had stolen 1s (5p) from her purse and wanted to purchase a pint of milk to counteract the acid's effects. The farm could only offer up a gill (¹/₄ pint) which he bought for three halfpence and stood in the farmyard to drink it. From here he walked to Rotherham and found himself lodgings for the night.

After a restless night Roodhouse decided he needed to tell someone of the murder he had carried out twenty-four hours earlier. At 1.30 pm on Sunday afternoon on 1 August, he arrived outside his aunt's, Mary Jane Hill house, at East Dene. Sitting on the grass bank about forty yards away from the front

Hooton Roberts today. The Author

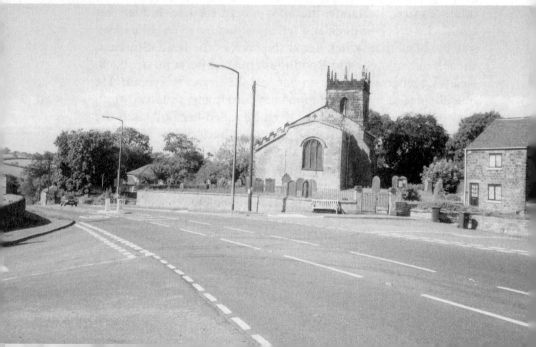

door he wrote a brief note and asked one of the children playing around him to take it, along with the empty bottle of salts, across to his aunt and ask if she would send some milk for him to drink:

> *Please let Edgar come up. I want to talk to him because it will be the last time I shall see him. I am going to give myself up to the police because I have done Kathleen in and she lies in Hooton Woods.*

As Mary Hill read the note, she looked out toward her nephew still sat on the grass bank, then gave the child a half pint of milk to take across to him. She was uncertain as to what her best course of action would be. If the note, or rather its meaning, were true, then she felt it unwise to approach him. Instead, after deciding not to send Edgar out to his brother, she took both the note and the bottle around the corner to Francis Barker to let him make the decision as to what to do next.

Francis, having read the few scribbled lines, shared her view but was somewhat disbelieving of his nephews ability to kill his own sister. He decided to walk over to Fitzwilliam Road and ask Minnie Hampstead's husband, who he knew to own a car, if he would drive him to Conisbrough and try to verify whether or not Kathleen had at least gone off with her brother. Once they realised this to be true they both went to Hooton Roberts and began a search of the woods but found nothing.

Meanwhile, Cecil Roodhouse had taken himself off from East Dene. After realising he was not going to see his brother he decided there was no point remaining outside the house. Beside which he also knew that the note would, at some point, bring the police. So, to avoid any further aggravation he calmly walked into Frederick Street Police Station in Rotherham and told the desk sergeant that he had killed his sister. After being cautioned he then made a full statement and later that same afternoon took police officers to Hooton Cliff Wood. The body was quickly found, as was Kathleen's parcel of clothes and as the the day came to a close Cecil Roodhouse was charged with murder.

The inquest, which was something of a foregone conclusion, opened at Rawmarsh council offices on Tuesday, 2 August. A large crowd, mainly of women, gathered outside in the hope of seeing Cecil Roodhouse arrive. They were to be disappointed because Cecil Roodhouse did not attend. It had never been the intention to bring him to court at this stage. The opening of the inquest was merely to allow Kathleen's body to be released for burial and a date was then set for a resumption.

The funeral took place on Thursday, 4 August at Conisbrough Cemetery amidst a crowd of over two thousand people, most of whom surrounded the small courtège as it made its way through the village, then stood in silence as the family gathered at the graveside. No doubt a fair number of those who attended the funeral also returned to Rotherham five days later in the hope of catching a glimpse of Cecil Roodhouse as he was brought from Leeds to Rotherham court house. The proceedings though were short. Roodhouse was remanded for a week whilst enquiries continued. So again many of those who had stood outside in the warm sunshine made their way across town to Rawmarsh where it was hoped he would attend the resumed inquest which opened that same

Cemetery Chapel, Conisbrough where Kathleen Roodhouse is buried. The Author

afternoon. Again they were disappointed. Roodhouse had been taken back to Leeds and his place filled by Keith Roddis, solicitor acting on his behalf. The hearing took evidence from both the family and police and after four-and-a-half hours the jury of nine returned the inevitable verdict of '*wilful murder*'.

One week later the West Riding Police Court at Rotherham, again swamped by a huge crowd, spent two hours sifting the evidence of Cecil Roodhouse's guilt and committed him for trial on a charge of murder.

The trial began in earnest on 7 December 1926 when Roodhouse stood before Justice McCardie at Leeds Assizes. He pleaded 'Not Guilty' to the charge. From the outset it was the defence intention, led by Mr Streatfield who had been appointed by the court, not to offer any evidence in support of Cecil Roodhouse. Instead he would challenge the prosecution case and attempt to prove insanity.

In this he was only partially successful. After hearing evidence of the murder and the state of Kathleen Roodhouse's body when eventually discovered, the court was told of the items found upon Cecil when he was arrested. He still had his sisters handbag, her hair slides and a pocket diary. This last item was his own and it showed for the first time the state of his mind after he had attacked his sister. He had made one significant entry:

> *There were five of us in the way - Cecil, Marcia, Edgar, Aubrey and Kathy. That is two of us out of the way – Kathy and Cecil.*

According to his defence counsel this entry had to have been made after the murder and whilst he waited to die believing he had committed suicide by swallowing hydrochloric acid. Had it not been for his lack of scientific knowledge, so the argument ran, the substance he bought on the day of the murder would have been something far more deadly. The entry then would have been read after his death and anyone reading it would have drawn the only conclusion available – that he was insane when he carried out the killing. It was a powerful argument.

Mr Streatfield then did his utmost to show madness, or at least that a type of insanity ran through Cecil Roodhouse's family. During cross examination of his mother, Eleanor Roodhouse, he raised the issue of her sister:

Streatfield:	*I believe you have a sister who has been confined to an asylum for some time –*
Eleanor:	*Yes*
Streatfield:	*Do you remember what age she was when she first went there?*
Eleanor:	*She was twenty four.*
Streatfield:	*The same age as Cecil?*
Eleanor:	*Yes.*
Streatfield:	*Do you know what is wrong with her?*
Eleanor:	*She suffered from a clot of blood on the brain and had pains in the head.*
Streatfield:	*Has Cecil complained of pains in the head?*
Eleanor:	*Yes.*
Streatfield:	*Have you been alright in that respect?*
Eleanor:	*No, I have suffered from pains in the head.*
Streatfield:	*In addition to that I believe your father suffered in much the same way?*
Eleanor:	*Yes, he had epileptic fits.*

There was never any suggestion Cecil had suffered epilepsy but clearly there was a suggestion he had been suffering mentally. The defence continued this line of questioning during its cross examination of Dr James John Hargan, house surgeon at Rotherham Hospital. Though the doctors evidence was only to confirm Roodhouse had swallowed a quantity of hydrochloric acid he was strongly pressed with regards to his state of mind.

Streatfield:	*You will agree with me that the mere fact that a man appears to be sane after committing some violent act and after attempting to take his own life is no criterion that he was sane at the time that he committed the act?*
Dr Hargan:	*That is so.*
Streatfield:	*In fact probably the shock of the act would bring him to his senses.*

Dr Hargan:	*Yes.*
Streatfield:	*Or the relief which may be experienced by a man who has had something on his mind for some time?*
Dr Hargan:	*Yes.*
Streatfield:	*So that the mere fact of subsequent sanity is not by itself a test? You have to look deeper?*
Dr Hargan:	*Yes.*
Streatfield:	*If a man murders someone of whom he is intensely fond, for no conceivable motive, it makes you immediately think - what was his state of mind when he did it?*
Dr Hargan:	*Yes.*
Streatfield:	*Is it possible for a man insane to commit an act and then when he recovers his sanity to remember what he has done?*
Dr Hargan:	*Yes.*
Streatfield:	*So that the fact that he has made a statement to the police about what he did, does not necessarily mean that he is sane?*
Dr Hargan:	*It is no criterion one way or the other.*

Defence counsel continued along this line with Dr Worsley, the Medical Officer of Armley Gaol, despite the fact he was in court to disprove Roodhouse's apparent insanity. It was the defence's claim that Cecil Roodhouse was suffering from Melancholia at the time he attacked his sister. Under a searching cross examination by Mr Streatfield, Dr Worsley was forced to accede to the defence barristers assertion that Roodhouse was not in possession of his mental facilities when he picked up the stone that was used to strike Kathleen on the back of her head, that he had no motive to murder.

Streatfield:	*Would you agree....that the lack of motive is the first indication of insanity?*
Dr Worsley:	*Yes.*
Streatfield:	*That depression and melancholia lead on to adolescent insanity?*
Dr Worsley:	*Yes.*

There followed a flurry of question and cross question from both defence and prosecution but the seed had been planted, though Mr Justice McCardie in his summing up told the jury melancholia was no crime or justification for murder. He held a view that insanity had not been proved in this case, rather this was a murder carried out through despair. The jury took half an hour to agree with him and Cecil Roodhouse was condemned to death.

But the judge's summing up gave hope to those who ardently believed he was suffering from a mental lapse that caused him to kill a woman for whom he normally held a high regard. A petition was raised within the week promoting Mr Justice McCardie's view that despair led to a period of insanity, that this meant the true verdict should have been, 'guilty, but insane'. Over three thousand people agreed with that view and put their names to the petition that circulated around both Denaby and Cadeby collieries, which were the nearest to Eleanor Roodhouse's home in Conisbrough.

Meanwhile an appeal was launched and heard on the 22 December. It found an unsympathetic hearing. The appeal court judges found nothing in the trial or the way it was conducted to overturn the verdict, so sentence was to remain in place. Cecil Roodhouse wrote a last letter home expressing his sorrow for what he had done and asking the family to visit him one last time. His mother launched a last ditch appeal to the Home Secretary, refusing to give up hope. It paid dividends, this along with the petition raised caused a change of heart. Cecil Roodhouse received his last minute reprieve and the death sentence was commuted to life.

Chapter 16

A Consequence of Theft – Agnes Taffinder
1934

Forty-four-year-old Nora Janet Taffinder was a devoted daughter and a conscientious worker. She rented Kenmuir House in Ramsden Road, Moorgate which she shared with her seventy-eight-year old, semi-invalid mother and her long term unemployed brother. For her, life, at its very best could only ever have been described as harsh. The only wage earner, the family had to consist on the 35s (£1.75p) she brought home each week and an additional 10s (50p) from her mother's weekly pension. Her brother Frank Taffinder, Jack to his friends, had not worked for four years. If Nora did not maintain this regular income, no matter how small, they would all find living at Kenmuir House more burdensome than it already was.

Being the bread winner brought with it not only the burden of financial responsibility but also a degree of moral accountability, particularly with her mother being unable to manage her own life unaided. By the early summer of 1934 Nora was finding both to be onerous, though money, or rather the lack of it, caused her the greater worry of the two.

In her role of shop assistant for Russum's on Bridgegate, she handled money every day and having worked there for the last seven years she was trusted. In the spring of 1934 she decided it would be simple enough to steal money if she stole in small amounts. How small depended largely upon the day's takings. For a month or so all went well and no-one appeared to notice these small amounts of money disappearing. Her confidence grew and she began to increase the amounts from a few pennies to a few shillings. By the end of May she had become very accomplished at adjusting the day's till receipts and this over confidence led to her inevitable downfall. On 9 June she

Bridgegate in the 1930s, by J Simonton & Sons. Russum's shop can be seen in the foreground. Rotherham Archives and Local Studies Library

slipped 5s (25p) into her bag. It was a larger than normal amount but she had no reason to suppose anyone in the shop entertained a suspicion about her honesty. She was wrong, Ralph Russum, a director of the company had apparently been suspicious of her honesty for some time. Seeing 5s suddenly disappear forced his hand and he called in the police. Nora was immediately interviewed by both he and the local PC. She never denied their allegation and admitted to the thefts. Distraught at her discovery and her culpability she admitted not only that day's theft but all the others. The company fired her on the spot and she was taken into custody. For Nora it was the end of her world. To be convicted of theft was tolerable, for her mother to be made aware was not. She insisted police did not visit her home and readily agreed to return to the police station on 13 June to be summarily charged.

With police agreement, she returned home feigning sickness and the need to take a few days off work. It was a perfectly rational excuse which the family had no difficulty in accepting. They knew well enough how hard she worked keeping the house running, she had suffered illness in the past and taken time off work as a result. For Nora, if it did nothing else, it bought time. Time in which she hoped to find a solution to a set of problems she had never anticipated.

As if to lend credence to her supposed ill health Nora Taffinder ignored the house for the next two days. She carried out few of her normal routines choosing instead to lie prone on the settee in a stuporous state. Frank Taffinder became concerned, neglecting the house in such a manner was far from normal. In none of her previous illnesses had she done that. Convinced she was becoming depressed he talked her into seeing a doctor. To support her pretence she agreed and returned from her appointment carrying a bottle of tonic prescribed to lift her spirits. For brother Frank it did the trick. Next day Nora talked of taking her mother to the Lake District for a few days holiday. Believing she was recovered from what ever malaise had afflicted her Frank readily agreed, suggesting Nora write to family friends in Keswick and make arrangements to stay with them. It was agreed between all three that Nora and her mother would travel the following week. The letter of course was never posted.

But both Frank and his mother believed, as Nora intended them to, that the planned holiday had helped shake off the despondency she had displayed since the weekend two days earlier. She worked hard to reinforce this belief, became more talkative, took up her household chores again. For Frank the house had returned to its familiar routines, something lost had been rediscovered, or so he believed.

On 13 June Nora did as she had agreed to do and arrived at Rotherham's Police Station at 10 am to receive a formal summons to appear before magistrates the next day. Police described her behaviour later as distressing. She thanked them for their kindness in not visiting the house and explained her excuse to the family for being at home. It was clear to the officers dealing with her situation that she was under considerable strain but there was little they could do to ease her pressures. But she returned home around lunch time seemingly well composed. Perhaps even a little self satisfied. Visiting the police station that morning had brought the urgency of her problem into sharper focus. For her at that moment in time there could be only one solution to the difficulties she found herself in. Calmly she sat at the kitchen table and wrote three letters, one to her brother Frank, one to close friends of the family and one to Ralph Russum enclosing £25 which she believed more than covered the thefts she had made. The letter to Frank she held back, the other two she posted then waited for night.

The sleeping arrangements at Kenmuir House were that she shared a bedroom with her mother whilst her brother slept in the back room. At a little after 11 pm Frank retired to bed. Nora remained downstairs as was her normal practice. When satisfied the house was quiet she wrote a short note for Jack, which she placed on a chest of drawers at the bottom of the stairs along with the letter she had written to him earlier, she took a razor from the bathroom and went to join her mother in bed.

At 3.45 am Frank Taffinder awoke to a strange, unfamiliar sound. Throwing the bedclothes off his bed he quickly went out onto the landing where her met Nora. She told him their mother had suffered a nasty nightmare, not unusual, and so after a little reassurance he returned to bed. He slept until around 6 am when Nora walked into his bedroom and told him that because she could not sleep anymore she was going downstairs to start her chores for the day. She went on to say that their mother was to have breakfast in bed and she would wake him again at around 7.30 am. He dozed for about half an hour then heard a noise from the kitchen downstairs which he thought to be Nora shouting out. Hurriedly pulling himself back out of bed he went down to investigate and found his sister slumped in an unconscious heap on the kitchen floor with the gas cooker fully on. Turning the gas off at the mains he dragged her quickly out into the hall way where he noticed for the first time the note and a letter both addressed to him.

Ramsden Road today. Kenmuir House has been renamed. The Author

Nora by this time was delirious but semi-conscious and as she regained consciousness began to ramble about their mother. Though her speech was somewhat slurred enough words tumbled out in a clear enough form for him to realise she was trying to tell him that mother was dead. Immediately leaving

her where she lay and still ignoring the letters he ran back
upstairs and into his mother's bedroom. She was, as Nora had
said, clearly dead, her throat slashed open, his discarded,
blood-stained razor on the floor beneath the bed.

Returning to Nora he dragged her into the front room and
ran out into the street to rouse his neighbours. They in turn
called for the police and the nearest doctor. Whilst all this was
going on Frank Taffinder took the two letters from the hallway
and sat down to read them. The first, a folded note, the one he
was supposed to have seen as he reached the bottom of the
stairs that morning, simply told him not to enter either the
bedroom or the kitchen before summoning help. The second in
its sealed envelope gave Nora's reasons for committing murder:

> *Dear Jack,*
>
> *I am sorry to leave you this mess, but I don't see any other way
> out. I have to go to court tomorrow for taking money and I
> cannot let mother face it. You can always be sorry for anyone
> now. I can tell you the suffering is beyond anything you can
> think of. I don't know what you can do, but perhaps someone
> will share the house and pay you a little. I should destroy Blackie*
> [the cat] *don't give him away. I am not blaming my employers.
> I expect I shall get blamed for other things now. I wonder if
> regrets come to everyone too late. Well you must make the best of
> things. I have sent Russum's £25 out of my own bank book.*
>
> *Now please don't have any regrets. I am glad to go, and I
> think mother will be better off. I thought how bad she looked
> today. I should get the rent paid and then you are all right for
> the house. I think the only things owing are the weeks meat...I
> don't want a sermon read over me. Please no flowers and bury
> me as cheap as you can. I have put out some sheets and pillows
> in the box just inside the box room. My bank book and the house
> book are just inside the drawer...You must not blame Russum's.
> It is my fault no-one else's...I don't think mother suffered much.
> Please forgive me, I am afraid it will be awful for you. I have
> hardly slept since Saturday, but I know what I am doing.*
> *Good-bye*
> *Nora*

Dr Coldray, the nearest GP to the house arrived at around 7

o'clock. Nora by this time had stumbled back out of the front room and was back in the kitchen trying desperately to inhale gas by whatever means. Belligerent and distressed she fought desperately to prevent the doctor removing the flexible gas pipe she had connected to the cooker from her mouth, totally unaware the gas had been turned off. It took a considerable amount of time to calm her and walk her back out of the kitchen into the front room. Then, leaving Frank to tend her as best he could, Dr Coldray went upstairs to examine Agnes Taffinder's body.

She was obviously dead, her throat having been cut and all the main arteries severed, though he noticed little bloodstaining. Deciding not to disturb the body in anyway he returned to Nora. By now the police had arrived and his patient was showing some signs of recovery. There was no doubt in his mind the woman was deranged and unsafe to be left alone at any time. He took the decision to admit her to Alma Road Infirmary where he knew her needs could be better catered for. Inspector Higgitt, senior officer at the scene accompanied her by ambulance.

On 22 June she appeared before Rotherham Police Court charged with *wilful murder*. No evidence as to Nora's state of mind was allowed at this hearing. The court's function being only to assertain her guilt or otherwise. The evidence as to her culpability was overwhelming. The letters alone confirmed premeditation. All were reproduced in court and had there been no other evidence these alone would have damned her.

Inspector Higgitt, who had attended her that night at Alma Road told the court that despite his insistence she say nothing, Nora refused to remain silent. She seemed to desperately need to tell him about what she had done. According to the statement she made whilst being transferred to hospital she had waited until her mother had fallen asleep then taken the razor and slashed her throat. It was at that point, she went on, that her mother had made the noise that awoke Jack in the next room. Having left her bed to reassure him that all was well, Nora then returned to lay beside her dying mother for a further two hours, never once looking at her, simply waiting for her death. From that point on she hoped her own death was a reassuring certainty. Jack's interference, however, ensured it would not be.

Inspector Higgitt went on to tell the court that in the examination he carried out at the house he found that Nora Taffinder had made every possible precaution to ensure her suicide was successful. The doors and windows had been carefully blocked and had she not shouted out whilst losing consciousness, she would almost certainly have died in the kitchen.

The court had little choice but to commit her for trial at Leeds Assizes on two charges, that of murder and of attempting to commit suicide. She pleaded not guilty.

The trial opened on 23 July before Sir Malcom Martin McNaughton KBE. Nora Taffinder was represented by Mr Streatfield whose intention from the outset was to prove insanity brought about, not merely through her loss of face at work, but through years of neglect. She had been, he declared, a devoted daughter, who had been used, as a slave by the mother she adored. As the trial progressed he constantly returned to this theme. Brother Frank taking the stand allowed him to develop the idea that Nora had led a fairly desperate life, not through abuse in a physical sense but through abuse in a mental sense. Nora, he claimed, had been used not only as sole breadwinner, but as nurse, maid, and charwoman. That throughout most of her life she had enjoyed no social intercourse in any way, shape or form. Mentally she had been under pressure to run a household without adequate support for much of her adult life. Frank Taffinder, through the answers he gave to defence questioning, helped support this view.

There was almost a lull as details were given by a series of medical men appertaining to the state of the body post-mortem and of the wound Nora had inflicted. Then attention once more returned to Nora's state of mind. Streatfield called the first of two experts in the field of mental health. Firstly Dr McDonald, Medical Officer of HM Prison Manchester where Nora had been incarcerated since the Rotherham hearing. He confirmed that in his opinion Nora Taffinder was mentally unstable; that since her arrival in Manchester she had at times sat wringing her hands whilst weeping or laughing out loud in a disturbing fashion. Her depression, according to his testimony, was still clearly evident:

Streatfield:	*Would you say she thinks she was perfectly justified in killing her mother?*
Dr McDonald:	*Yes - on the last occasion I saw her she did not seem quite so sure but all the other times she has been quite definite.*
Streatfield:	*Has she shown any remorse?*
Dr McDonald:	*She has always discussed it quite calmly.*
Streatfield:	*In your View she knew the nature of her act?*
Dr McDonald:	*Yes.*
Streatfield:	*Can you form an opinion as to whether she thought it was wrong?*
Dr McDonald:	*I think she did not know it was wrong.*

Next came Dr Charles Donaldson Law who gave corroborating evidence. His view left no doubt in anyones mind, Nora Taffinder had no conception of right or wrong. When she murdered her mother, he testified, she believed her actions were justified in order that her mother be saved the inevitable anxiety that would follow, once knowledge of her court appearance for theft became known. His opinion of the killing was:

...she had found an insane way out of her difficulties and her mind then became relieved. Her stress disappeared because she had found a way, which was to kill her mother and then kill herself.

Any uncertainty in the defence case was swept away by this single opinion. In his summing up to the jury Justice McNaughton told the jury that when any individual killed another in the full knowledge of the nature of the act and in the knowledge that it was a wrongful act, then they were to be regarded as sane. If on the other hand the opposite were true then that person must be considered insane.

It was a point not lost upon the jury. They had listened

intently to the detail of the murder and the testimony of the two examining doctors. There was no doubt in their minds that when Nora Taffinder took the razor to bed with her that night it was not to commit murder as she saw it, but to end the anxieties she felt would beset her mother were she to have been made aware of her own crime of theft. They took only fifteen minutes to return the verdict that had become more and more inevitable as the case progressed – 'guilty of murder but insane'.

Chapter 17

The Cost of a Mug of Water –
Jack Wright Burrough
1940

ack Wright Burrough had a serious speech impediment. At times it rendered him incapable of holding an effective conversation. His schooling had been somewhat retarded as a result and as he reached his twenties he began to drink. Alcohol countered his sense of inferiority, created in his mind a greater equality than he would otherwise have felt. By the time he had reached the age of twenty-four he was known as a hardened drinker.

On the night of 28 June 1940 he walked into the *Thurcroft Hotel* at 7 pm. It was Friday night and as usual the promise of a good night ahead. For the next two and a half hours he, along with a friend, Michael Keating and a man known as Finney, discussed the war in detail. At certain points during their conversation Burrough became very animated. Club steward, Thomas Handley, had to warn him to keep his voice down. It made little difference to Burrough who by 9 pm that night had consumed some eight pints of beer. At that point he and Finney left the hotel and walked across to the Colliery Institute. Here they stayed until just after 10 pm. By this time both men had consumed a good deal of alcohol. Finney suggested they go back to his house, and Burrough readily agreed.

The Thurcroft Hotel, *now known as* The Thurcroft. The Author

Orchard Lane at the top of which once stood the Stray's Farm. The Author

According to Finney's wife Sarah, Burrough was by far the worst for wear when they both walked into her kitchen. She made him tea and he played checkers with her children for half an hour or so then left. Being drunk meant going home was not an option so he walked back to the *Thurcroft Hotel,* though it was less to do with alcohol and more to do with conversation that took him there; but club steward, Thomas Handley just wanted to wash up and get to his bed. The conversation, what there was of it, was brief. Because of the amount of alcohol Burrough had consumed by the end of the night Handley would not serve him and told him to go home. But going home was still not an option. Instead he decided to do as he had done on similar occasions. He walked to Orchard Farm at Thurcroft where he knew he could either sleep off the night's exesses in the barn or wrapped up inside a hay stack. He had known John and Lucy Stray who owned the farm for many years. Lucy Stray had been one of the few people to not show impatience at his speech impediment and as a consequence was one of the few people he had befriended. Though the couple never knew of his nocturnal habits, using their outbuildings he considered to be perfectly acceptable. Unfortunately this night, unlike any other was to prove disastrous for all concerned.

At around 11.15 pm, having tried to settle in the barn, he was being kept awake by thirst. He knew there was no water pump in the farmyard, so he struggled to his feet, walked over to the farmhouse and knocked on the door. The Stray's had been in bed since 9.30 pm. John Stray was sound asleep until awoken by his wife pushing herself out of bed to go downstairs. He heard her open the backdoor then scream loudly. Throwing the bedclothes back he ran downstairs as best he could. As he walked into the kitchen he caught sight of the back of Burrough leaving by the door. Thinking quickly he slid the bolt and turned the lock before trying to help Lucy who was prone, lying on her back on the kitchen floor. Still conscious but bleeding from the nose and mouth, he tried to pull her across the floor toward the foot of the stairs but the effort was too great for a man in his seventies. Realising he was not going to be able to drag her upstairs he fetched a bowl of water and using a flannel tried to clean her wounds. Burrough meantime came back to try and force the door. Unable to break in he then went to the window at the front of the house. John Stray aware of what he was trying to do went to the window to prevent him forcing his way in. At that point Burrough smashed through the window using a wooden cudgel or some sort of garden implement then ran off down the garden path. John Stray closed the blind and made another attempt to move his wife. Still unsuccessful he then heard Burrough return to the window and pull the blind from its wall fixings. Now fearful for their lives John Stray struggled back up the stairs, flung open a window and started shouting for help.

Harry Webb and a few men from the local Home Guard heard his shouts and ran across to help. By this time Jack Burrough had fled the scene. After searching the barn they in turn called out a doctor and Lucy Stray was carried upstairs.

Orchard Farm, loaned by Patrick Donlan. The photograph shows the farm and outbuildings as they were at the time of Lucy Stray's murder. The Author

According to Dr Kemp who examined her she had a fracture of the right jaw, considerable bruising to the mouth, nose and eyes. At the time he carried out his examination she was semi conscious. He left instructions with John Stray as to what to do through the night and left. An hour later Lucy Stray's condition had deteriorated to such an extent Dr Kemp was recalled but it was too late. Lucy Stray had died from a haemorrhage to her brain.

Jack Burrough, unaware of what he had done, made his way home. But having been seen not only by John Stray but also by the local beat bobby who saw him making his way toward the Orchard farmhouse at around 11 pm, he was not to sleep soundly in his bed. Police arrived at his door at one thirty that morning. After denying he had anything to do with what was now being considered a murder, he agreed to go with officers to Orchard Farm. After being shown the damage to the window and reiterating his earlier denial he was allowed to return home. But not for long.

By 4 am police had concluded an intensive search and

assessment of damage to the farm. They were able to show that twelve of the sixteen panes of glass that made up the front room window had been smashed. A garden syringe was discovered outside the window and marks on the window sill suggested this was used to carry out much of the damage. Fibres were found on the glass fragments still in place and on small pebbles on the living room floor.

At 5 am Burrough was re-interviewed and his clothing seized for forensic testing. He again denied any involvement in the crime insisting he had returned home after a night's drinking. But this time there was irrefutable evidence placing him at the farm. Fibres from his jacket matched those found on the glass, pebbles found in his jacket pocket matched those found in the front room, as did glass fragments and pieces of putty. In the right cuff of his jacket and in the turn-ups of his trousers were found leaves from a Rosemary bush matching the bush outside the farm window. He had skin missing from the knuckles of his right hand and a blood-stained handkerchief in his trouser pocket. If nothing else this mounting evidence forced him to re-think his denials and he duly confessed.

What Jack Burrough did not do though was accept he had murdered Lucy Stray. According to the story he told police after wakening the house because he wanted a drink of water Lucy Stray filled a mug from the kitchen tap and brought it to him at the door. At that point, according to his version of events, he pushed his way into the house catching her in the process across the face. He saw her fall but did not hear her scream then went back out into the yard. He agreed he had thrown pebbles at the window and had broken a number of the panes but could offer no explanation as to why. He was duly charged with murder.

Committal proceedings commenced on 29 August at Rotherham West Riding Police Court. Jack Burrough, because of his inebriated state on the night of the killing, continued to plead not guilty to murder. It is possibly true that at this time he was still unsure of the events surrounding that night at Orchard Farm. The key debate in the courtroom centred around whether or not he had struck the blow that killed her or had she struck a piece of furniture as she fell?

Dr Hynes of Sheffield who had examined Lucy Stray after her death concluded that she had been struck, possibly by two blows to the head from a fist. He did not subscribe to the defence argument that she could have fallen against the corner of the table as she fell. He argued this would more than likely have left her with an open head wound, there was none. He was supported in this argument by police evidence that showed a trail of blood leading back from the doorway to the place on the kitchen floor where she fell. The jury concurred and he was found guilty and sent for trial at Leeds Assizes.

The trial opened on 26 November before Mr Justice Cassells. Jack Burrough was defended by Mr E Sykes who told the jury at the ouset it was his intention to show that at the time of the killing, Burrough was so far under the influence of alcohol as to be unable to form any criminal intention. Jack Burrough, he contested, had not attacked Lucy Stray but had killed her by accident.

There followed a series of witnesses who could verify to Burrough being drunk on 28 June. Not merely tight, or tipsy but being in a state of intoxication that would render him incapable of sound reasoning. In other words he would not have been aware of the impact his actions were to have. The court listened as those who spent the night drinking with him told their story, at the end of which there was no denying alcohol had played a large part in what took place at Orchard Farm the night Lucy Stray died.

When Jack Burrough took the stand this view was reinforced further. After five months he was still unsure of the events of that night. He could not remember whether he drank from the mug of water offered to him, nor could he recall hearing John Stray call out to him. He had little recollection of breaking the windows and continued to claim he had never deliberately struck Lucy in the face. According to his testimony it had all been an accident:

> I did not make any attempt at all to strike Mrs Stray...There was no reason why I would...I made a bit of a move like to walk into the house and I knocked her over...

Clarifying his point he said he had caught her in the face with his hand when he tried to enter the kitchen and as soon as he saw she had fallen over he left. But again he was unable to offer up any explanation as to why he then attacked the house.

Not a version of events the prosecution believed to be truthful, they brought a Dr Brisby to the court to testify to the injuries Lucy Stray had sustained. They intended to prove it could not have been accidental and was a deliberate, intentional, act. He certainly went some way to substantiate the defence argument. It was his contention that regardless of the amount of alcohol he had consumed that night he must have been aware of his actions.

Judge Cassells:	*You have heard how Mrs Stray's jaw was broken, her eyes blackened and that she died from these injuries. Is it your view that this condition of drunkenness would be such that he would not know he was striking her, assuming he did strike her, or would he know he was doing it ?*
Dr Brisby:	*If the fracture of the jaw was a result of a direct smash with the fist the man would know he was doing it.*

Mr Justice Cassells obviously did not accept this argument. In his summing up to the jury he told them that if it was their view that Burrough was so influenced by drink as to be incapable of forming intent then he could not be found guilty of murder. They agreed, returning a verdict of manslaughter. Judge Cassells, on passing a sentence said of Burrough:

Upon that night, by reason of excessive consumption of alcohol, you became a beast. You, a man aged twenty-four years, treated this woman outrageously. The court is bound to take a very serious view of what you did on that night.

Punishment – severe punishment – there must be, to you for what you have done and as an example to those like you who drink and drink until they can drink no more and then go out and do violence on inoffensive and defenceless creatures.

He was then sent to prison for seven years. Seventy-seven-year-old Lucy Stray had paid a heavy price for a mug of water.

Notes and References

1. John Whitaker inherited upon the death of his father in 1843.

2. William Harrison was Mayor of Rotherham twice, 1874-75 and 1879-80. He died whilst in office, in June 1880.

3. Rotherham's Workhouse was located off Alma Road. It was built upon five acres of land purchased for £1,000 in 1837, the land known at the time as Penny Less Walk Close. It was demolished when Rotherham's new hospital opened at Oakwood.

4. The Archer Family lived at 60 Moorgate, Rotherham, in a semi-detached house called Elm Tree House. The house stood on the corner of Alma Road and Moorgate opposite what is today the *Florence Nightingale* public house.

5. Police Constable Lewin Atkin was born in 1863 in Norton, Derbyshire.

6. The *Poor Prisoners Defence Act*, 1903, allowed those on a charge of murder access to public funds to assist in their defence if their earnings were deemed insufficient. It was repealed in 1967.

7. Sergeant George Brookes, born 1853, served twelve years in the 2nd Royal North Lancs Rgt of Foot, joined Rotherham police in 1881 and was promoted to sergeant in August 1889.

8. Amy's father was William Beckett.

9. The Stainrod house still exists as one of a terrace hidden behind the *Sir Colin Campbell* pub.

10. Edwin Weatherhogg joined Rotherham police as a constable in 1887, becoming Chief Constable in 1907.

11. Thomas Firth [1789-1850] founded the company in 1842. It was incorporated as Thomas Firth and Sons in 1881 – *Giants of Sheffield Steel* (Geoffrey Tweedale) (1986).

12. Rose Proctor had her sentence commuted because she was found to be pregnant. Walter Gibbin was never executed but no record exists of a reprieve therefore it is likely he died whilst in prison.

13. Alfred Bostock was born Alfred Davis.

14. Board of Guardians were formed in 1834. They were an elected body, one man representing each parish or district of the town. It was their role to distribute relief to the poor – Judith A Shearer, *The New Poor Law Act*, (1967).

Index